A Culture of Agency

Other Redleaf Press books by Lisa Burman

Are You Listening? Fostering Conversations That Help Young Children Learn

A Culture of Agency

Fostering Engagement,
Empowerment, Identity,
and Belonging in the
Early Years

LISA BURMAN

Redleaf Press®
www.redleafpress.org
800-423-8309

Published by Redleaf Press
10 Yorkton Court
St. Paul, MN 55117
www.redleafpress.org

First edition 2023
Cover design by Danielle Carnito
Cover photographs by jovannig / Ann Radchua / Rawpixel.com / stock.adobe.com
Interior design by Wendy Holdman
Typeset in Adobe Text Pro and Supria Sans
Printed in the United States of America
30 29 28 27 26 25 24 23   1 2 3 4 5 6 7 8

Library of Congress Cataloging-in-Publication Data

Names: Burman, Lisa, author.
Title: A culture of agency : fostering engagement, empowerment, identity, and belonging in the
     early years / by Lisa Burman.
Description: First edition. | St. Paul, MN : Redleaf Press, 2023. | Includes bibliographical
     references and index. | Summary: "Using her everyday research approach, in the tradition of
     the pedagogistas of Reggio Emilia, author Lisa Burman observed several special classrooms
     and identified some common threads: engagement, agency, identity, and belonging, which
     together combine to create what she terms a culture of agency. The term agency is widely
     used, but often misunderstood as "giving children choice." Agency is far more than this,
     and the most powerful learning happens when personal agency is connected to community
     agency: we are only as strong as each other"—Provided by publisher.
Identifiers: LCCN 2022061774 (print) | LCCN 2022061775 (ebook) | ISBN 9781605547985
     (paperback) | ISBN 9781605547992 (ebook)
Subjects: LCSH: Student-centered learning. | Early childhood education. | Agent (Philosophy)
     | Belonging (Social psychology) in children. | Identity (Psychology) in education. | Choice
     (Psychology) in children.
Classification: LCC LB1027.23 .B87 2023 (print) | LCC LB1027.23 (ebook) |
     DDC 371.39/409678—dc23/eng/20230209
LC record available at https://lccn.loc.gov/2022061774
LC ebook record available at https://lccn.loc.gov/2022061775

Printed on acid-free paper

For Sienna, Evie, Layla, and Quinn:
May you continue to love learning and discover what brings you joy.

A child must have some version of,
"Yes, I imagine I can do this."
And a teacher must also view the
present child as competent and
on that basis imagine new possibilities.

—Anne Haas Dyson, "Coach Bombay's Kids Learn to Write"

Contents

Acknowledgments

I love the writing process, and I love teaching young writers. Still, it's a little nerve-racking when you finally make your writing public and share it with the world. Old doubts emerge, and I wonder if what I have to say is really worth listening to. Thankfully, I have an amazing support network that stops me from being paralyzed by self-doubt. I'm indebted to them all for their kindness, encouragement, and wisdom and for the time they gave to supporting this project. I know my writing is richer because they were there for me.

First and foremost, I must thank the talented educators who inspired this book and generously shared their teaching with me, providing the stories you are about to read. Without your contributions, this would be only half a book. You welcomed me into your preschools and classrooms so I could research your intentional teaching. And when COVID-19 restrictions kept me out, you wrote your stories and met me on video calls so I could continue the research. What a gift! Thank you for your time, openness, and generosity and for continually inspiring me as an educator. Sending my respect and gratitude especially to Marcia Fraser, Megan Fyffe, Erin Gracey, Amber Hall, Kylie Pollard, Danni Porcaro, Henry Sheedy, Philomena Scrafton, and Liesl von der Borch.

Thank you also to the preschools and schools that generously invited me to be part of their journey, made me feel welcome, and gave me a sense of belonging. A special nod to Cathy and children from St. Margaret's Kindergarten for the fabulous videos of their agentive outdoor learning. I extend my gratitude, particularly, to the leaders of three learning communities in Adelaide, South Australia, whose stories fill these pages: Ngutu College, St. Paul Lutheran School, and Prospect North Primary School.

To my team—where do I start? Being a consultant without a community of one's own can be lonely. Every day, I'm grateful that the universe brought us together and we connected because of our shared values and belief in the capacity of young children. We're bound by our conviction that schools can do better for children. You make me a better educator and leader. I offer a huge thanks to each of you, not only for the stories and wisdom you added to these pages but also for the never-ending support and encouragement you provided so generously—Katie Ashmead, Amanda Bartram, Penny Cook, Dannielle Gibson, Mimi Hayward, and Angela Kernahan. Bring on Bali! A special shout-out to Amanda, who was my writing buddy for the first draft of this book, reading the messy first pages and giving the most helpful feedback.

I offer thanks to my other educational friends. To the "Booth Gals"—thank you for listening and believing and always supporting. Thank goodness for our agenda ritual, that's all I can say! To my good friend Matt Glover—your words as you left Adelaide the last time, "The world needs another Lisa Burman book!" spurred me on throughout the writing process. You have no idea how much your encouragement has meant to me. To my other educator friends, thank you for always showing interest in this project and offering support and encouragement: Tina Adamo, Jackie Becher, Helena Card, Vicki Froomes, Max Greenwood, Susanne Harding, Heather Jenkin, Diane Kashin, Leah Mermelstein, Kath Murdoch, Cathy O'Dea, and Alan Wright.

Thank you to Redleaf Press, and especially Melissa York, for believing I had another book in me. (Maybe there's another one yet?) Thank you for championing this book, dealing with all my Aussie spelling and grammar, and nudging me along to be a better writer.

A massive thank-you to my family and honorary families. I'm blessed to have parents and a sister who always believe in me and support all I do. I give a nod to my other constant writing buddy, Scout the miniature schnauzer, who mostly slept in her bed beside my desk, but who always kept me company as I wrote. I'm doubly blessed because of the friends who are like family and who are always there for me. You know who you are. A very special thank-you to Caroline and Neville Fergusson for the roof over my head and so much more.

Finally, to the children who helped me fill these pages with their marvelous words and ideas—you inspire me to be a better human as well as a better educator. My work is all about you and making schools better places for you to thrive.

Introduction

You know it when you see it.

You know it when you *feel* it.

It's hard to define and put into words.

What makes this classroom work so well? Why does it feel different from other learning spaces? What is that buzz you feel as you enter? And—most importantly—how do we create this environment for *all* children?

I have so many questions when I enter learning spaces like this. My curiosity is sparked. But what accounts for the dramatic difference in these preschools and elementary classrooms compared to others I visit? What theories do I have—or can I create—about why there is such a difference? Even describing the difference can be elusive; it is quite abstract. You can feel the energy for learning, but you can't touch it. It's a feeling as much as an intellectual knowing. Surely this learning culture does not only spring up spontaneously, so how can it be cultivated on purpose?

Let me paint a picture that will put you inside one such learning space. I'm sure you'll recognize it. Perhaps it is your space or that of a teacher you have long admired. Of course, each early learning setting will be—and should be—unique. I'm not advocating for a cookie-cutter approach at all, but there are common flavors you will recognize.

Danni's Young Authors

It's a cool but sunny winter's day in Adelaide, South Australia. I quietly enter the Year 2 learning space to collaborate with the educator, Danni. Twenty-five six- and seven-year-olds are gathered in a circle in the meeting area. Danni is seated on the floor as part of the circle. The children have their bookmaking folders in front of them and are quietly talking with each other. There is a sense of calm anticipation as I join them. Danni chats with the children near her and catches my eye with a smile. "Lisa is here now, every-one," Danni says in her usual quiet, clear, and gentle tone. "So, we're ready to start our writers' meeting."

The children immediately turn to greet me with big smiles, a friendly "Hi, Lisa" here and there, and a few waves. Then they turn to Danni. They know what will happen next. Danni will lead them in a conversation about something important to them as writers. They'll listen to her, talk with a partner, and share some thinking. On this day, they are wrapping up a study in which they have created fantasy picture books, so they talk about what they need to do to be ready for the publishing celebration in a few days' time. I hear the children share their thinking:

> "I'm nearly finished revising. I've added the detail and the color. I think I'll be done with that today."
>
> "I'm editing today. I'll ask Dash to help me because he's good at making books."
>
> "I've done the editing. I'm ready for a conference, Danni."

As the writers' meeting ends, the children (actually, they would tell me to call them "writers" or "authors" in this context!)—the *young authors*—move off to find a place to work on their books. There is no running or bumping or jostling for a position or for materials. Within a couple of minutes, all the children are engaged in their writing, collecting materials to help them with their writing, or having one-on-one conversations with Danni.

There is a quiet hum as some writers talk with each other. Some choose to work solo, finding a private nook to write in where they won't be dis-turbed. Some writers choose to sit at tables, and others huddle on the floor with miniature tray tables to lean on. Danni sits on the floor in the meeting area, conferring with two children.

The children are self-directed and independent in their learning, but there's something more that I struggle to put into words. It feels almost businesslike. The young writers are all involved in an endeavor that is worthy of their time, and they seem to know it. Their actions proclaim, "We have important work to do here."

I chat with several children during their writing workshop that day. I usually start by asking something like, "What are you working on?" and then inquire about their writing process: "Where did you get this idea?" or "What did you work on in this book to make it interesting for your readers?" or "Show me a part you're really proud of" or "What's your next step?"

I am blown away! I cannot wipe the smile off my face. These young writers can really talk about writing. They share their thinking and their intentions. They are aware of their audience and the genre they are writing in.

> "The robot had this problem here. See? This is where his arm breaks off. So then he has to work out how to fix the problem. And he does that at the end."

They use specific metalanguage to tell me how they want to excite or scare their readers:

> "I did big and bold [letters] here because I want the reader to say it like this . . ."
>
> "Here is when the zombie gets scared and runs away. It's funny, not scary, so I did the zombie's face looking really funny so my reader will laugh too."

This hum of activity continues for a full forty minutes before Danni gently asks everyone to finish and to bring their bookmaking folders to the reflection circle, reminding them, "As you come to the circle, you'll be deciding what thinking you want to share about your writing today."

This vignette doesn't show Danni's skills in "behavior management" (a concept I'm not too fond of anyway, as we want children to manage their own behavior). It's not a story of "well-behaved" or compliant children. It's not even about how Danni is an expert teacher of young writers (although she is). This is a story of *engagement*, *agency*, *identity*, and *belonging*.

Use this QR code to view a video of part of a writing workshop in Danni's class. You'll see the engagement, self-direction, and purposefulness of the young authors.

https://www.youtube
.com/@prospectnorth
primaryschool3025
/featured

Everyday Research

In my work, I have the honor and privilege to be invited into learning spaces like Danni's, where children of all ages are deeply involved in their learning. Learning isn't something that is done *to* them. It is what they *engage in*. They have a say in it. They are in the driver's seat. They care about their learning. I imagine the neurons in their brains firing as their ideas spark up and as they actively think and stretch themselves intellectually.

Children being actively involved in their own learning does not mean there isn't a strong and important role for the educator. In fact, nurturing this level of participation requires the most sophisticated teaching we can engage in. The writing workshop I was lucky to witness is only a very small part of the story. Danni's class did not magically work like this from day one of the year, and they don't only think and act this way during writing workshops. Everything Danni does as an intentional educator enables learning like this to happen every day in many contexts.

So that's how this book began. I was so excited by the powerful learning and engagement I *felt* in Danni's classroom that I could not stop thinking about it. What made Danni's classroom so different from others I visited? What did she do—and not do—to create such a strong culture of learning?

I had some theories. I wondered if Danni was even aware of the transformative things she did for the young learners in her care. My gut feeling (another way of saying "theory") was that the first weeks of the school year were critical. I decided I wanted to research this. I'm not an academic, so my kind of research is what I call "everyday research," the kind of research educators practice day in and day out: reading, viewing, observing, listening, and engaging in dialogue. It's the kind of research that Carla Rinaldi, from Reggio Emilia, speaks of when she says this (quoted in Edwards, Gandini, and Forman 1993, 244–45):

> When teachers make listening and documentation central to
> their practice, they transform themselves into researchers. . . .

Only searching and researching are guaranteed to lead us to that
which is new, that which moves us forward.

I invited a small group of fellow educators along for the ride, and I am
indebted to them for their generosity and openness. You'll get to know them
a little through the stories on these pages.

My research began by asking questions:

- What do teachers like Danni do during those critical first
  couple of weeks of the new school year?
- What *don't* they do during that time?
- How do they structure their days in the first few weeks?
- How intentional are they in planning for and building a
  culture of agency and learning?
- How do the children feel about being part of their learning
  community, preschool, or classroom?

This book is a synthesis of what I discovered from my everyday research.
I'm so grateful to the educators who supported my process. They welcomed
me into their teaching and into their thinking. They openly shared their
hopes, dreams, intentions, and frustrations. I hope you too will learn from
their wisdom as I share glimpses into their intentional teaching.

I've synthesized our collective thinking into a framework that can be
used for imagining, enacting, reflecting, and evaluating (diagram I.1). This
book won't cover everything there is to say about building a strong learning
culture—it's too rich and complex a topic for any one book. But I hope it
can bring some clarity to the kinds of actions and intentions that are important to give time and attention to, things that might not be explicitly stated
in a national curriculum or set of standards and things that aren't assessed
in any high-stakes test. But these things are so important that they make all
the difference in learner engagement, agency, identity, and belonging, and
therefore to well-being and learning.

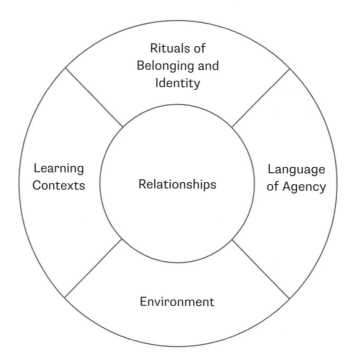

Diagram I.1
A Framework for Building a Culture of Agency

Five areas emerged from my everyday research:
1. Relationships
2. Rituals of belonging and identity
3. Language of agency
4. Environment
5. Learning contexts

In designing the framework, I knew it needed to be simple but not simplistic. A framework helps us organize our thinking around a big concept, and so, I believe, it needs to be simple to be the most useful. But this does not mean it is simplistic in the thinking it holds within each component. Creating a culture of agency requires complex, flexible, and sophisticated teaching and, therefore, the same kind of thinking.

We can plan intentionally for each of the components. Many educators already do this, and many do so unconsciously. When we raise the planning to a more conscious level of thinking, it will only become stronger, deeper, and more intentional. By learning from the sophisticated teaching of the educators I researched, we can all become more purposeful in our planning for culture building instead of beginning each year, term, or semester just as we've always done. I decided to place relationships in the center of the framework to show that everything really comes back to this. Teaching is one of the most relational professions that exist. We can plan for relationship building, just as we can for the other components. At the same time, the components of ritual, language, environment, and contexts help build relationships.

How This Book Is Organized

We'll begin by exploring what a learning culture is and what research says is important to any culture building. I'll describe what I mean by an *agentive culture* so you know exactly what I'm hoping this book will help you build with your young learners. We will also take a look at the complex teaching required to be attuned to culture building, because it's so much more than planning an effective lesson or providing a beautiful play invitation.

Then we'll explore each of the components in the framework individually: relationships, rituals of belonging and identity, the language of agency, the physical and temporal environments, and learning contexts for agency. Each component is brought to life with stories from real early childhood settings, educators, and children ages three to eight. You'll learn strategies that you can put into action straightaway or, better still, modify and tweak to make them your own.

Chapter 7 touches on educator agency. Without experiencing (and using) agency as educators, creating an agentive culture for children is difficult. I wonder if many educators struggle to define and create such a culture because they have not experienced it themselves, instead facing mandates to follow a scripted program or curriculum models that take away their agency and creativity as educators.

Finally, we'll end with a reflection and goal-setting tool to help you connect to your own values and learning philosophy. Guiding questions will help you identify the kind of learning culture you want to create and make plans to be more intentional in this, no matter what time of the year you begin. Each section of the tool could also be used for facilitating reflection and dialogue at your team meetings or professional learning communities (PLCs).

You'll find QR codes sprinkled throughout these pages. These will lead you to a video that brings the ideas we've just explored to life. I hope that seeing and hearing possibilities will deepen your understandings and inspire you to reflect on your own context. These videos are not intended to say, "This is how your context needs to look," but to act as inspiration and a provocation for your own goal setting.

I want to note the language I use in this book. I intentionally choose the words *child* and *children* over *student* and *students*. I don't judge anyone who uses the word *student*, but I decided almost two decades ago to use *child* because it feels more aligned to my beliefs and values. I believe that education is for and about the whole child, not only the academic ("student") part of them. I choose to see children and educators as competent and full of potential. This view builds on strengths. The opposite view sees children and educators from a deficit stance, either as needing to be fixed or as empty of prior learning or experiences of value. The word *student* seems to place limits on seeing both children and educators as whole and competent people for me. I will also use the word *school* inclusively to represent all school settings, from prior-to-school settings such as early childhood education and care settings, preschools, and kindergartens to primary and elementary schools. While most of the stories I share will be from Australian preschools and primary schools, I believe the lessons from these teachers and children apply to all age ranges and school settings. In Australia we have many names for the first year of primary or elementary school and also for the year prior. In South Australia, where the schools in this book are situated, we tend to use *preschool, kindergarten,* or *kindy* for the year prior to primary school (typically for children aged four and turning five). Our first year of primary school (five-year-olds turning six) is named "Foundation" in our national curriculum but called "Reception" in my state. I've endeavored to keep the language as consistent as possible to help your reading have clarity.

I have chosen to use non-gender-specific pronouns when appropriate. Where I have used a gender-specific pronoun, it is because I know the educator's or child's pronoun preference. Finally, I use the terms *teacher* and *educator* to refer to all adults working with children in school settings, inclusive of co-educators, teaching assistants, class-based teachers, curriculum or site leaders, and specialist teachers.

Let's begin!

CHAPTER 1

What Is a Culture of Agency?

When I started writing, the culture of learning I wanted to examine seemed far too rich and beautifully complex to be limited to a one-word label. I'm still not entirely confident that the word *agency* suffices. But I hope that in exploring what agency means, this book will provide an expansive and luxurious definition of the word and, therefore, illustrate what it looks, sounds, and feels like in a preschool, classroom, or school.

Can you recall the picture I painted of Danni's writing workshop in the introduction? If not, take a few minutes to reread that section. I want you to have a mental image as you read this chapter. Even better, in rereading my description, bring to mind a learning environment you know where children and educators are engaged in the abundant life of learning together.

Now, with that image in your mind, we'll engage in some everyday research. What words would you use to describe this setting? Spend five minutes brainstorming words and phrases. Don't filter or organize your list (you might want to do this later, but not now).

Here's my list—unfiltered and unorganized:

- joyful
- businesslike
- active
- talk
- purpose
- engagement
- independent
- collaborative
- self-directed
- respectful
- children's voices heard more than teachers'
- light touch
- relationships
- nudging
- celebrating
- children learn from each other
- hands-on experiences
- listening

- interest in children's ideas
- democratic
- participation
- interdependent
- community
- identity
- thinking
- theories

- wonderings
- curiosity
- confusions
- risk-taking
- problem solving
- confidence
- acceptance
- decision-making

As I reread my list, I notice that some words are directly observable (*active, hands-on experiences, children's voices heard more than teachers', independent*). Some are learning dispositions (*risk-taking, participation, curiosity*), and many are values (*acceptance, democratic, respectful*). I think most educators would identify these ideas when naming the culture they wish to create, but some educators are more successful in building this culture than others.

Let's unpack some of the key ideas, starting with the big one: agency. We could shelve this away as just edu-speak or one of the current catchphrases that we hear at conferences or in professional articles. It will be a great shame, however, if we only think of it as the latest fad or slogan, as I believe understanding what agency is (and isn't) can help us identify the kind of learning community we want to create with and for children.

I believe agency is within us all. Babies are born with an inner drive to connect with others. It is not something they are explicitly taught. In this sense, teachers can't *give* children agency (like giving them a choice in materials to use), but we can create the conditions for children to feel a sense of agency in their learning—or not. This is the culture we build in our preschools and classrooms.

In her book *Wellbeing from Birth*, Rosemary Roberts (2010, 188) sees agency as the "feeling that you can make a difference to your own life, and to the lives of other people." As the COVID-19 pandemic hit in 2020, many of us felt a loss of agency as we were forced to live in ways that diminished the human experience of community and the richness of our previous lives. Our ability to make certain decisions was taken from us: we could no longer travel or visit family and friends or perhaps go to our workplace. The limitations impeded our rights as citizens, and they also affected our emotional sense of having control of our lives, as the future was unknown and many of our choices were removed. This lack of a sense of agency led many to feel as if we had no say in our lives, that things were just happening *to* us and we had no power to control or influence them.

Thankfully, as I write this book, many countries have been returning to greater normality, or what many call a "new normal." With this comes a return of control over our lives; we can plan for the future with hope and know we can again set goals and have power to achieve them.

Take a few minutes to return to the brainstorming list you created at the start of this chapter. How would you sort and categorize the words? How do they connect to Roberts's definition of agency? How do they connect to your personal experience of agency in your life? I blended and organized my list of words into the following areas to better understand and articulate this culture of agency I envision. I discovered that many of the words belonged in more than one category, showing the interdependence of many of these ideas in creating a culture of agency. They do not operate in isolation but are integrated and connected in the daily fabric of the preschool or primary classroom.

Belonging and Identity
joyful, respectful, celebrating, relationships, children learn from each other, interdependent, community, identity, acceptance

Engagement and Participation
joyful, active, talk, purpose, engagement, independent, collaborative, self-directed, children learn from each other, hands-on experiences, participation, thinking, theories, wonderings, curiosity, confusions

Self-Efficacy
businesslike, purpose, independent, collaborative, self-directed, interdependent, risk-taking, problem solving, confidence, decision-making

Democratic Values
active, talk, purpose, respectful, children's voices heard more than teachers', light touch, listening, interest in children's ideas, democratic, participation, community, acceptance, decision-making

Belonging and Identity

The desire to feel a sense of belonging is part of the human condition. It doesn't matter if you're an introvert or extrovert; we all have an innate urge to seek and create belonging. Babies are born into the world seeking connection, and we live our lives finding it through our families, friends, work, learning, the arts, playing, sports, and hobbies. Identity and belonging are intertwined. We build our sense of ourselves through our connections and interactions with others. Our belonging informs our identity.

Where do you feel most yourself? Where do you gain your sense of belonging? For me, I feel this most with my family, with my closest friends, and also when I'm collaborating with like-minded early childhood educators. I feel simpatico with my colleagues, but it is more than that. With them, I have the confidence to be myself, to take risks, to show who I am as an educator and a human being in all my messy complexity.

We build our sense of who we are through our interactions with the world, and particularly our interactions with others. In an early learning setting, the relationships a child builds with educators and peers are the glue that binds everything together.

Belonging to any group or community brings with it responsibilities and boundaries. There are certain ways of being that are expected by the group, and there are some actions and words that are not encouraged or even accepted. For example, if you belonged to a scouting organization or a sporting club as a child, you can probably recall the expectations and rules of the group. In my childhood netball club, if you didn't come to Thursday afternoon training, you weren't picked for the Saturday team. My friend's book club meets monthly in different members' homes and, apart from an expectation that you've read at least part of the selected book, members place a big emphasis on the kind of cake the host bakes. No store-bought cakes allowed! So, when we talk about belonging, we also need to consider boundaries. I find boundaries to be much more meaningful than rules because they are connected to the desire to belong. They build security and trust. They enable us to be vulnerable and to truly be ourselves.

Imagine for a moment that you're in a new professional group, one that you don't immediately feel a connection with. Perhaps you have a real-life experience to draw upon, like starting work at a new school or with a new team. I remember one time when, at a large conference, I was put into a random group with educators I had no connection with. I held back my participation, even though the topic was something I had experience with and knowledge about. I chose to remain silent. In this situation, I was given the opportunity to use my agency and participate, and even to initiate a new thread in the conversation, but I didn't use it. I didn't yet feel safe enough to be vulnerable and reveal a bit of myself to that new group of people.

When adults have a strong sense of ourselves within a group—that is, when we experience secure identity and belonging—we are more likely to use our agency to fully participate. The same is true for children. With a strong sense of belonging and identity, children will have the confidence to contribute their ideas, knowing their thinking will be respected by the adults and children. With boundaries of belonging, children will trust the relationships within their group or class. Trust builds the security they need to feel safe to initiate their learning. When children feel they belong for who they are, they are free to act on their ideas without fear of judgment or reprimand. This creates an emotionally safe environment where children's agentive drive takes full flight.

Engagement and Participation

We often use the word *engaged* to describe learners, but how do we know when a child really is engaged in learning? From the outside, it isn't easy to work out whether a child is actually hooked into the learning or merely going through the motions. Some children have perfected the art of looking engaged while they are really pretending to learn. They have learned to do what the educator wants (for example, being quiet and still, or completing the task, or cooperating with others by always agreeing), knowing that nothing more will be asked of them. It is impossible to see agency in action when children are pretend learning. Pretend learners are compliant, allowing learning to wash over them rather than becoming fully involved and using their agentive drive to participate and contribute. They feel things are done to them and do not recognize their internal power to make things happen. Unfortunately, in education, engagement is too often confused with compliance.

Ferre Laevers, from Leuven University in Belgium, has been instrumental in helping educators understand deep involvement (or engagement) in learning. His research (2005) resulted in an educational model for preschool called Experiential Education and identified these indicators of involvement:

- intense concentration
- managing distractions
- persistence
- intrinsic motivation
- energy and drive to explore
- complex and creative thinking

Totally involved learners operate at the edge of their capacity in their zone of proximal development. They push themselves to the outer edge of their limits. They are highly motivated to continue learning because they are interested and feel success. Motivation is driven from within. This is when we see agency in action.

The most engaged learners understand that learning requires some effort and have learned to become comfortable with the uncomfortableness of learning. If we are not a little uncomfortable in learning, we probably have not reached our zone of proximal development. Instead, we are learning within our zone of actual development, which helps us to gain fluency, automaticity, and confidence but will not stretch and engage us in new learning. The same is true for our professional learning. I call this a "wonderful uneasiness." The uneasiness nudges us further or deeper into our understandings, and the wonderful part comes once we realize how much we've grown as educators.

In the year of writing this book, 2022, my friend and colleague Katie and I have been talking about the idea of feeling uncomfortable in learning. We noticed a pattern in many of the classes we visit that sparked our curiosity: more children seem to be stuck in their comfort zones and are not willing to stretch themselves, when we know they are capable of more. We wondered:

- Is this related to the past two-plus years of living with COVID-19, where children's families and the world sought to keep them safe, so children did not take many risks in learning and play?

- Has having high expectations, the intent of which is seeing the child as capable, been misinterpreted as pushing the child? In trying to avoid pushing, have families and educators been too hesitant to nudge, suggest, and encourage? (To us, a *nudge* is asking, "With a *little bit* of teaching, what will the child be able to do on their own?")
- In wanting to encourage and respect children's ideas, have educators been afraid to take a more active role, therefore accepting children's mediocre efforts?

We don't have answers to these questions, but our theorizing helped us clarify our observations and better understand the "itch" that was under our skin. We were curious and a bit puzzled, and we wanted to understand what might be happening. We needed to "scratch the itch." This is when a reflection or observation makes you pause and ask yourself, "Hmm . . . I wonder what's going on here?" or "This doesn't feel quite right. Is there a different way to think about this?" The itch of curiosity is where our everyday research often begins.

Katie decided to respond with the class of seven-year-olds she was teaching by explaining the zones of proximal and actual development with them. Once children understand the zones of development, they are very capable of using the framework to reflect on and plan for their learning processes and experiences. A simple diagram like the one following (diagram 1.1) can help children understand that sometimes the learning will flow and feel easy. This is learning in the *practicing zone,* where we build fluency and confidence with ideas and skills we already know. Other times, learning will feel more difficult and a little trickier. We might have to put more effort into figuring out a problem or trying a different way. We will have to be resilient and persistent to keep trying in different ways, keep thinking about the idea, and not give up. When we are in the *learning zone*, we are building our "learning muscles." When we are in our *stretch zone*, the learning feels too hard for today, but that doesn't mean it will always feel that way. By stretching ourselves and trying new things, the learning will move from the stretch zone to the learning zone.

The teacher creating an agentive culture makes time to explore the zones of learning at the beginning of the year and returns to them during the year.

But just showing the diagram and talking about it with children is insufficient. Rather, we need to use the framework in our own reflections about our learning. We might use words like, "I had to work hard to figure out how to draw the horse in my book/practice the guitar/knit this sweater, but I kept trying different strategies. So I think this is in my learning zone. I didn't give up, and now I feel a sense of satisfaction and pride that I could do it."

We can also use the framework to name children's learning processes: "I can see that you're trying different ways to get that block to stay on the very top. You're in your learning zone! You're building lots of strong learning muscles by not giving up and trying different ideas."

Or the framework can help children prepare for certain learning experiences: "Most of us will be in our practicing zone today because this number game is helping us to build our fluency and confidence with the numbers we know." Or "This is a new idea for lots of us, so you might feel as if you're in your learning zone as you explore and make today. What will help us learn as we're in our learning zone, particularly if we feel a little stuck?"

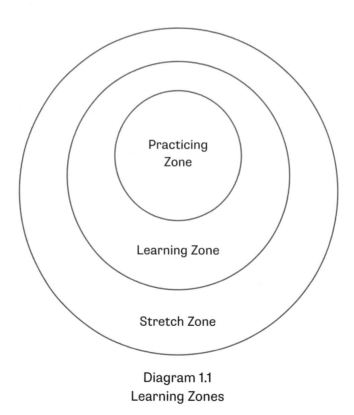

Diagram 1.1
Learning Zones

The work of Mihaly Csikszentmihalyi (1979) on the idea of *flow* also helps us understand the difference between engagement and compliance. When we are in flow, we are completely absorbed in an experience. Yet flow isn't always quiet and peaceful. The children in Danni's class weren't quiet or still. There was energy, movement, and a buzz of talk in the room. But they *were* engaged. They blocked out the distractions of others moving and talking around them to focus on their bookmaking. I believe many of them likely were experiencing a sense of flow and were totally absorbed in their experience.

Your Everyday Research
Pause and reflect on the children in your site.
- ▶ When and where do you see indicators of involvement or engagement (as listed on page 6)?
- ▶ Where and when are the children most engaged?
- ▶ When might they just be going through the motions?
- ▶ What is it about a learning experience that creates the conditions for involvement, or not?

Self-Efficacy

Albert Bandura (1977) used the term *self-efficacy* to describe a person's belief in their ability to succeed in a particular situation. It is more than feeling good about yourself, however, because self-efficacy is connected to some kind of action. Self-esteem is your sense of self-worth. Self-efficacy is your perception of your ability to achieve a goal. It starts with being able to imagine you can do something. It's that deep "yes I can" belief in yourself. But it is also more than being motivated. Motivation is a *desire* to achieve a goal, whereas self-efficacy is a belief in your capacity to achieve this goal *and* having the skill set and disposition to do so. I can *want* to run a marathon, but without the self-efficacy of believing I am capable of it, and then committing to the training required, it will remain just a dream. (By the way, I don't feel at all capable of running a marathon, so it will remain a dream just on these pages for now! No self-efficacy in marathon running for me.)

Self-efficacy is connected to many concepts we are already familiar with in education: growth mindset, intrinsic motivation, and metacognitive awareness. Self-efficacy helps us work out

- the goals we want to pursue (What is worth putting effort into?),
- how we go about achieving those goals (What strategies will help me?), and
- how we reflect on our progress (How am I doing?).

Self-efficacy is at the heart of experiencing agency in our lives. The opposite is mindless compliance and obedience.

For a moment, imagine a preschool or school where children do *not* experience self-efficacy and agency. Here children are governed by many rules the teacher has set. Children can use only the materials presented to them. They are not permitted to move materials to different areas or pick out something themselves. The children follow directions. They ask for permission for the simplest of things, like what they can write or if they may have some tape for their construction. The learning experiences offered to them may be interesting on a certain level, but there is little room for the children's ideas, thinking, or curiosity. The learning is prevented from going on tangents or following the children's lines of thinking.

When children and adults have lived within a non-agentive culture (let's call it a "compliant culture") for a long time, it disempowers and de-skills them. They not only stop believing in their own capacity but also lose the skills and strategies they need to be agentive. A new educator in this environment who seeks to create more opportunities for children to experience self-efficacy will likely meet some initial bumps in the road. Simply asking children to make their own decisions, to lead their own learning, will be like pulling the rug out from under them.

I've worked in some of these compliant cultures, endeavoring to open educators' thinking to the capabilities of children to think, create, question, wonder, and theorize. It's hard work at first. The children have not developed strategies for problem solving or planning their learning. They often ask for permission to do things or for reassurance that what they are doing is okay. Children who have lived in compliant cultures do not know that adults are interested in their ideas and thinking and so keep them to themselves.

They often respond with what they think are the "right answers," and when the questioning becomes more open-ended or meandering—pondering and wondering about theories and ideas—they feel lost. They do not know how to have these kinds of beautifully messy conversations and learn with others.

This causes me great sorrow, because I believe that children are born with agency and a strong urge to explore and learn. Some education systems have squashed this exploratory drive from children, just as Sir Ken Robinson, in his famous TED Talk, warned how "schools kill creativity" (Robinson 2006). Of course, I do believe there is a way out of this situation, and that is why I'm writing this book. I hope it will give educators and schools a map for finding our way back to the agentive child.

Children who live and learn in cultures that support a strong sense of self-efficacy and agency

- develop a deep interest and curiosity in learning,
- show stick-to-itiveness and a commitment to learning experiences,
- show resilience in the face of setbacks and challenges,
- seek intellectual challenges and enjoy thinking hard about things, and
- initiate their own learning.

See videos of the outdoor learning at St. Margaret's Kindergarten, Woodville, South Australia. You'll see self-efficacy in action as these four-year-olds gather resources, use a variety of learning strategies, and support each other in pursuit of their own play goals.

https://youtu.be /U81Cyd2V9Xs

Democratic Values

Returning to my brainstorming list, I pull out my final group of words— *active, talk, purpose, respectful, children's voices heard more than teachers', light touch, listening, interest in children's ideas, democratic, participation, community, acceptance, decision-making*—which I classified under "democratic values." They're not all values, of course, as some are observable actions like *children's voices heard more than teachers'*, but to me they embody an understanding of power that provokes helpful reflections for educators.

The etymology of the word *democracy* is Greek, from *demos* ("the people") and *kratos* ("to rule"). So, *democracy* means "rule by the people." In a democratic society, people have the power and opportunity to participate in decision-making. Democratic political systems have sophisticated voting systems to ensure everyone has a voice and the opportunity to participate in the decision-making of the country or organization (even if they choose not to use it). Members of legislative bodies are elected by the people to represent their perspectives and to be their voice in government. The power of decision-making is therefore shared. The opposite is a society where power is held by one person or group, as in a dictatorship. In nondemocratic cultures, those who have power hold it over other groups, whose voices are silenced or not sought. They do not have the opportunity to participate in making decisions that affect their lives.

Pause for a moment and consider what you think about when you hear the word *power*. Is power something external or internal? What can the word *power* mean? The *Oxford English Dictionary* offers this definition: "the ability to control people or things." Its etymology comes from Latin and French roots, with meanings related to having great strength or being capable of exerting great force. We also use *power* when referring to electricity, *powering* our lights and appliances. We talk of *losing power* when there is a blackout. In this way, power can be a source of energy, and it can be turned on or off. I would like to offer other ways of thinking about power in our roles as educators. We can have *power over*, and we can have *power within*. Let me explain.

When we feel a loss of agency, like when the COVID-19 pandemic affected our lives so severely, we may feel that power is being held over us or taken away from us. When an early learning setting places too many restrictions and demands on children—when educators are dominating and, for example, children need to ask for permission to use materials or can only participate in the experiences set up by the educators—they are experiencing power being held over them. This power is external and controlling. The children's internal power has been turned off.

However, when we think of power as an internal force, an internal energy to be and to do, it opens possibilities for how we can help others use their internal energy. This is what is meant by *empowering*. The agentive learning culture we hope to create empowers children to use their internal energy to engage in learning: to do, make, create, move, problem solve, make decisions, sing, dance, and live and learn fully. Within a culture of agency, educators exert their energy to turn on children's internal power to shine!

There is one other way we need to think about power in this culture of agency: as *shared power*. We can think of *shared power* as a democratic value because it enables many people to participate in decision-making, rather than leaving the power with only one person or group. To fully embrace the idea of sharing power in our early learning settings, we must reflect on and understand our own view of children. This is an idea I first wrote about in *Are You Listening? Fostering Conversations That Help Young Children Learn,* inspired by my long-term study of the educational project in Reggio Emilia. Our internal (and sometimes unconscious) image of the child affects everything we do:

- Do we see children as innocent and so need to protect them from harm and wrap them in cotton wool?
- Do we see children as empty and so believe our role is to fill them up with knowledge and develop a certain set of skills?
- Do we see children as a threat to our power and control as educators or parents? When we feel that our own power or authority is threatened, we often resort to placing more controls and restrictions on children.
- Do we see children as inherently filled with potential and capable of incredible learning? Are we fascinated by their learning processes and believe they have something worthwhile to contribute?

An image of the child as strong and capable is a belief in the fundamental worth and dignity of every person. It is at the heart of an education that supports the values of democracy. These can be understood as values that make society fair and include the following:

- Participation. The right to have a say and participate in decision-making that affects you.
- Respect for and appreciation of diversity. Supporting cultural diversity and diverse ways of learning and thinking.
- Fairness and equality. The understanding that we all belong to our society and community and we have responsibilities to each other.
- Truth. Being open to exploring big ideas with children because this honors the human experience.

Democracy is embodied in article 12 of the United Nations' Convention on the Rights of the Child: "Children have the right to say what they think should happen when adults are making decisions that affect them and to have their opinions taken into account" (UNICEF Australia, n.d.).

Internal Control

When we believe children have something to say worth listening to, when we are interested in their ideas, we also see that they are capable of sharing power and having a say in their lives and in their learning. In early childhood settings, this belief comes to life when children and educators collaborate, negotiate, and respect each other's ideas.

The setting that seeks to create a culture of agency will not impose endless rules and regulations on children. The educators will not use modes of discipline that exert power over children. They will not use extrinsic reward systems like stickers and behavior charts to get children to comply. These are another form of external control. Instead, educators work hard to help children develop an internal locus of control, where children believe they can make things happen. With the opposite—with an external locus of control—children believe things just happen *to* them. Yes, developing agency and internal control can be the harder, and sometimes longer, road to take.

Stickers and reward charts might bring about immediate compliance, but they only help in the short-term. The longer and harder road will pay off immeasurably in the end, as children will believe in their own internal power for self-efficacy: to initiate learning, make decisions, resource their learning, and problem solve. They will become more deeply engaged in learning and in the life of school, because it has personal meaning and relevance.

Educators who create an agentive culture understand that the boundaries that come from belonging ("because you belong here") are far more effective than those based in having power over someone ("because I said so") (Roberts 2010). As Daniel Pink (2011, 108) writes in his fabulous book about motivation, *Drive: The Surprising Truth about What Motivates Us*, "Control leads to compliance; autonomy leads to engagement."

Within a culture of agency, educators think it is important for children to have and make choices about their learning and everyday life and to share in the decision-making of the class or preschool. The child's right to have a say in their learning also brings with it responsibilities to each other and to themselves. Once again, we see how important the value of belonging is. From a strong sense of belonging, children build understandings of what it means to live and learn in a community: they come to know that their ideas are valued and listened to and that they share responsibility for the well-being, happiness, and success of the group.

Creating an agentive culture calls educators to pay attention to the relationships they build, to the ways they create a sense of identity and belonging within the class or group, to the language they use to empower children, and to the ways they curate an environment to fully engage children in initiating and directing their own learning.

Sometimes thinking about what something is *not* helps to crystallize what it *is*. The following chart shows some of the distinctions between a culture of agency and a culture of compliance. Of course, it is not as cut-and-dried as this chart—real life looks more like a continuum. Reflect on your own pedagogical decisions in terms of aiming to do less in the "Culture of Compliance" column and more in the "Culture of Agency" column.

Culture of Compliance	Culture of Agency
Children are viewed as innocent and needing protection or seen as a threat to adults' feelings of control.	Children are viewed as fully human, with ideas, theories, opinions, and feelings that are to be listened to and considered.
Teaching is viewed as filling the child with knowledge and developing skills for a particular purpose.	Teaching is seen as understanding, scaffolding, and expertly guiding children to form conceptual understandings and to develop skills and strategies that can be transferred.
Children are expected to follow the educator's instructions without question.	Children's interests, wonderings, and confusions drive the learning. Children have a say in their learning so it is meaningful to them.
Children are expected to ask for materials and do only the tasks set by educators. They are not permitted to move materials from one area to another.	Children have autonomy and self-efficacy to access materials and direct their own learning within boundaries or guidelines set by educators.
Children are seen as followers or receivers of learning experiences that are decided upon by the educators.	Children are seen as active participants and initiators of learning.
Extrinsic motivational strategies such as stickers, charts, and rewards are used.	Intrinsic motivation is valued over extrinsic rewards. Educators work hard to offer learning experiences that are meaningful and relevant to children so they want to actively participate.

CHAPTER 2

Relationships Are Everything

I have been fortunate to have many fine educators in my life. Some of them have imprinted in my memory more than others. One of these teachers is Mr. Niven, my Year 6 and Year 7 teacher, from way back in the late 1970s. What I remember most about Mr. Niven is not the math or history lessons he taught but the *feeling* I had in his class and the community he created with our group of eleven- and twelve-year-olds. I remember how he made me feel important and smart and capable of things I never thought I could do—even singing in a children's operetta performance! The memory I hold on to is how I felt *seen* and *known* in Mr. Niven's class.

Perhaps you're now recalling past teachers who saw you and knew you too. I hope so, because this feeling of being known and understood is so important in creating a culture of agency. Many of the following chapters will spiral back to the essential idea that teaching is all about relationships. The language we use, the rituals we create, and the environments we curate and maintain all play a large part in building relationships. In this chapter, we'll gain clarity surrounding the kinds of relationships we need to nurture and discover some strategies we can intentionally use in building them, particularly at the beginning of the school year.

Not all relationships are equal. We understand this because that's how life is. Therefore, it is critical to reflect on the kinds of relationships we build as educators. What kinds of relationships support children to feel a sense of agency and to be ready, willing, and able to initiate their own learning, rather than remaining passive recipients of what is offered to them?

Let's put ourselves in the shoes of a child beginning child care, preschool, or school and ponder what that experience might be like. As this child, you need to leave your primary relationships of family and home to enter a new place and be with people you're unfamiliar with. And you have no choice in this change—you must go to child care or preschool or school when your family sends you. I liken it to when I moved from Australia to New York. It was such an enormous change to be in a new culture in a city where I knew no one, working in an unfamiliar education system. It was highly stressful (as well as exciting). Yet I was doing this by choice, unlike when children go to child care or school.

Researchers from the University of Bath, led by Dr. Julie Turner-Cobb, studied the stress levels of children beginning school. They measured children's cortisol levels (widely known as the stress hormone) over several months as they began primary school. The researchers weren't surprised to find that children's cortisol levels were significantly high at the start of school, but they also discovered high levels of cortisol several months *before* starting school. This suggests that children are not anxious only as they begin school but are already feeling stressed about the transition during the lead-up to the big day (Economic and Social Research Council 2007).

Turner-Cobb's study showed that most children experience some level of stress when transitioning from preschool to school (or when entering a new child care room or new class at the beginning of the year). That's probably not a surprise to those of us who work with children and families during those transition months. When humans feel stress, the cortisol and adrenaline in the body prepare the sympathetic nervous system to fight, flee, or freeze. With stress hormones pumping through the body, it can be impossible to think deeply or be reflective. It can be difficult to get deeply engaged in an experience or stick to a task. Our nervous systems and our bodies just won't allow it because they're preparing us to respond to a perceived risk.

What does this mean for educators as they are welcoming children and families into their learning communities? Children in a new situation will often find it difficult to focus for long periods of time. They might find it difficult to fully engage and become deeply involved in learning experiences. They might not be able to draw on strategies for self-regulation and managing conflict, because their entire being is attuned to getting through the day in this new place and with these unfamiliar people. Some children will be hypervigilant and anxious about what is happening next because they are unable to predict the flow of their day or guess how unfamiliar people will react. We ask a lot of young children during these big transition times, don't we?

Given that picture, we as educators are called upon to create conditions where children's stress levels gradually subside so they can fully engage in learning and in forming the relationships that will be so important to them all year.

The Child-Educator Relationship

The relationship a child builds with their educator is one of the most significant connections in their life. As early childhood educators, we are often a proxy parent for children, particularly when we educate and care for very young children who are venturing out from the family unit for the first time. The attachment a child and educator build together is essential for the child to thrive at preschool or school.

Attachment theory offers us a helpful lens here. Attachment is sometimes confused with bonding and affection, which are part of it, but these are not sufficient to describe the depth of relationships with secure attachment. Attachment theory can help us understand what is happening—and where we should put our energies—in the first few weeks of a new school year or when a child joins a new child care group or school.

With that in mind, I'm drawn to the definition from one of the pioneer researchers on attachment, Mary Ainsworth (1967): "An affectional tie that one person or animal forms between himself and another specific one—a tie that binds them together in space and endures over time." In an educational setting, we're talking about a relationship between an adult and child in which the child feels secure and has trust in the adult, and which endures over time.

We can form attachments to people and also to places. Developing secure attachments with both educators and the educational space means children feel confident to actively participate—to use their agency—and initiate learning without fearing physical or emotional harm. They feel safe to be themselves and venture into the unknown of learning.

Educator Megan Fyffe pays a lot of attention to relationship building at the beginning of the school year. She prioritizes taking time to make each child feel special, supported, and seen by creating micro-moments of connection. This could be as small as a smile and nod when a child looks up from playing to check that Megan is still there, or sitting with a child during snacktime and chatting to get to know them a little more. It is necessary to spend time together to build positive relationships.

Megan knows relationship building is so important that it can't be left to chance. It is her number-one priority in the first week of school, so she plans for uninterrupted times of play, social interaction, and exploration, whether she is teaching children in kindergarten (called "Foundation" in Australia) or Year 3. We'll explore the learning environment more in chapter 5, but for now, it's helpful to see the connection between time and relationships. If Megan scheduled the day as a series of teacher-directed tasks, it would leave little opportunity for those micro-moments of connection. Instead, her days are more fluid, with ebbs and flows and a rhythm, but always with uninterrupted playtime.

Megan also schedules what she calls a "soft start" to the day every day. When she taught Year 3 children, the day began with fifteen to thirty minutes during which the children could choose how best to transition from home to school: by listening to music, drawing, chatting with friends, playing games, creating poetry, playing in the kitchen-play area, or reading. This sacred time gave Megan the opportunity to connect and build relationships with every child. It was not a time for administrative tasks but for checking in and gauging how everyone was that day.

Watch video of Megan's "soft start" to the day where you will see how Megan supports children to transition themselves from home to school.

https://youtu.be
/Sv5OD9nAJbo

Here are other ways to create micro-moments of connection:

- Spend each day sitting with a different group of children as they eat snack or lunch. Don't spend this time catching up on emails or putting up a display. The connection you'll make with the children by spending ten minutes with them— interacting socially just as you would with your friends over lunch—is much more important.
- Greet each child by name and give them a warm smile as they arrive. Let them know they are seen and belong here. Your

smile acts as a bridge so the child can move from the familiar into the unfamiliar. During one of my observation visits, I overheard Philomena greet a child who had been absent for a few days. "Oh, Jivin, I've missed you so much. I'm so happy you're back!" Imagine how welcome Jivin felt, how seen and known he felt, by hearing those words. He belongs there, and he was missed. This seems simple, but in the busyness of the day, these moments can get lost. Make it a priority.

- Avoid the pressure to begin assessments too early in the year or as a child enters your setting. First, a child under stress will not be able to shine, so you won't get accurate information. And second, your relationships are more important than any data you might collect. Instead, pay attention with all your senses. Observe children during the day and make anecdotal notes about their strengths and interests.

- A child does not exist in a silo. Show your interest in the names of their family members, including pets. It can be challenging to learn all the names of extended family members and pets in the first couple of weeks. My advice is to ask children about their families during your micro-moments of connection and keep notes. You could also send home an envelope containing a few small index cards, asking families to write the names of the significant people and/or pets in their child's life on each card. The cards can stay in the envelope or be put onto a key ring, which in turn becomes a transitional object or a set of high-frequency words to support the writing of older children.

- Share a little about yourself with children, as much as you are comfortable with. By knowing who your family is, if you have pets, or what you like to do on weekends, children will form a stronger connection with you.

- Return from your breaks in a timely way. Even if you're only a minute or two later than expected, children can begin to feel anxious that you are not returning. In the early days, you are likely to be their main secure relationship at school, as the children haven't yet had time to establish others. Even

if you have introduced the children to the teacher next door
or a co-educator, these relationships are not the same as the
primary relationships you are building with them, simply
because you've spent more time together. When you are
punctual and predictable in your actions, children will learn
to trust that you will always return, and their anxiety will ease.
Over time they will also build other relationships that support
and nurture them.

- Laugh with children. Having fun together binds people
  together. Find and share joy in the everyday, in picture books,
  and in jokes and songs. Dance, play, and be silly along with
  the children.

Now to a tricky question. What can we do when we find it difficult to
build that secure attachment and bond with a child? We're talking about
human relationships, after all, and they are complex and sometimes messy.
I think it's only realistic to expect that we will connect with some person-
alities faster than others—it's like this between adults, and I can't see why
it would be different between an educator and a child. What is different,
though, is that we are professionals working in service of children and families. We're called not just to accept a lack of connection but to keep nurturing a positive and respectful relationship.

My wise friend Dannielle Gibson nudges our thinking about this situation by asking, "Is this about the adult's perceived connection or the
child's?" How is the child feeling here? Do they feel the same sense of dis-
connection? Our priority must be the child's perception of being known and
seen, building that relationship of secure attachment no matter how long it
might take.

I recall a child I taught, many years ago now, with whom I found it
difficult to make a connection. They always felt a little distant from me.
And if I'm completely honest, there were plenty of days when I went home
exhausted from supporting their self-regulation (often not all that successfully!). I knew this child faced difficulties outside of school and there was
likely some trauma affecting their ability to form an attachment with me. A
strategy that I found helpful was to imagine the child *not* as someone who

always lost their lunch box, who found it difficult to sit and listen to a read-aloud, and who got into frequent conflicts with other children. Instead, I imagined the child as someone who was *learning* to look after their belongings, *learning* to engage with picture books, and *learning* ways to play and learn with others. I imagined and believed in the capable child. Slowly, not overnight, they developed strategies and dispositions for engaging in learning and, most important, they increased their trust in me.

Another wise friend and colleague, Penny Cook, empowers her child care and preschool team with a strategy for building connection with children. They focus on what the child is *seeking* rather than what the child is *doing*. This is such a powerful strategy for not defining a child by their behavior. All behavior is communication, after all. Penny leads her team in phrasing the intention as a "wondering." For example, when Sammy throws sand at Finn in the sandpit, the educator might say, "Sammy, I'm wondering if you're wanting to play with Finn? Finn, I think Sammy wants to dig too. Let's get a shovel, Sammy."

Just as with our adult relationships, some take longer to develop than others. The slower-to-develop relationships call us to be more intentional and to invest more time. It is only through shared experiences and many encounters that relationships can grow. Some strategies to try include these:

- Observe the child playing and notice what they are interested in. What do they seek out? Are there repeating themes to their play? What picture books are they drawn to? Then bring something connected to this interest into your site, perhaps a book all about lizards for Callum or items for a fairy garden with Mack in mind.
- Ask the child to help make a book about their favorite subject. You might suggest, "I really want to make a book about outer space, but I don't know much at all about it. I wonder if you would help me, Amira, because I know you know a lot about planets and the solar system."
- Choose to sit with the child during mealtimes over a number of days.
- If you work within a team, discuss the value of having each person spending time with the child intentionally. It may be

that the child is feeling overwhelmed by too many people, and nurturing each relationship over time will support secure attachment. This can become your research project, as you observe, theorize, try out, and reflect on ways to build a connection with the child.

The Child-Child Relationship

The friendships children build in preschool and school are some of the most significant in their lives. We learn so much with and from our friends. Many have the potential to become lifelong relationships that enrich our lives and build our identity.

Think about how some of your friendships grew. Friendships don't usually happen immediately but are built gradually over time and with shared experiences. You first meet, perhaps through an introduction, have some interaction, and find something in common. But you wouldn't say you are friends because you've only just met each other. At first you are acquaintances. You might immediately like each other, but it is only after repeated opportunities to meet and interact, each time learning more about each other, that the relationship develops into a friendship.

This idea has implications for the decisions we make in the first weeks of school. Just as Megan ensures a fluid day to allow for micro-moments of connection between adults and children, we need to ensure children have time and opportunities to build relationships with each other. This can't happen if the whole day is directed by adults. Uninterrupted time for playing, reading, talking, and creating together provides the opportunities for connections to be made and friendships to bud.

Not all child-child relationships will result in friendships. Isn't it interesting how adults often expect all children to be friends with each other? Why? Just because they are a similar age? We would never expect an adult to be friends with everyone in their workplace, but we can unconsciously put this unrealistic expectation onto children.

Apart from ensuring there is ample uninterrupted time for play and interaction, strategies for supporting child-child relationships, particularly at the beginning of the year, include these:

- Sing songs that include children's and educators' names, like "Hickety Tickety Bumble Bee" and "Willoughby Wallaby Woo." It is much easier to form relationships with people when you know their names!

www.youtube.com /RWEDUqO8oUg

- Play circle games that use children's names and also provide opportunities for children to interact with different children.
- Write each child's name on a card to spark curiosity about letters and words. The most important word in the world is your name! Play games with names, and sort them into different groups, such as beginning or final letters, number of letters, and so on.

www.youtube.com /watch?v=8P2LSww PBuo

- Invite children to help with special jobs in pairs to encourage new connections. For example, you could invite Johnnie and Mack to help set the table for lunch or to take food scraps to the compost bin. Their shared endeavor could well be the start of a new friendship.
- Attach photographs of the children onto wooden blocks. These can be included in block and construction play or in small-world play, or to show who is at school or at home today. Don't forget to add your image to a block too!

Living and learning in a community means members have responsibilities to each other. Although we understand that not everyone will necessarily be friends, we do expect civil and respectful interactions. A strong sense of belonging fosters these boundaries, but conflict is a natural and normal part of life. We all experience conflict, ranging from large and debilitating issues down to small annoyances. Given that conflict will always be part of life, helping children develop strategies for managing conflict is one of the most important things we do as educators.

Occasionally, I'll work with an educator who seems to get annoyed every time there is a moment of conflict between children. It's almost as if they expect children never to want to use the same bucket in the sandpit or to go on the swing when someone is already there. But this is life. Conflict will happen, and it's our responsibility to support children in these moments, not shy away from them or take over to solve them for children. If we sanitize or control the environment so much that children don't experience conflict, we hinder them in learning how to regulate big feelings and in developing strategies for resolving differences.

Instead of seeing conflict as an annoyance, the educator who seeks to create a culture of agency knows it is an opportunity for learning. I understand that the disagreement over the red car might be bothersome, especially if it's the fourth time that week the children have fought over the rights to the car. This conflict might interrupt something we are doing with other children or another planned experience. But this is when we need to step up, putting aside our personal annoyance and taking the opportunity to model and support the children in their disagreement. As Penny wisely says, "We're the grown-ups here." Remember that this car is the most important thing in the world to the children at this particular time. Cortisol and adrenaline are pumping through their bodies, impeding their ability to logically think through the steps to a solution. Strategies for co-regulating with children in stress is a topic of (many) other books, so I won't elaborate too much on this here. We'll return to the idea a little in chapter 4 when we look at the power of language in creating a culture of agency. If you would like to learn more about self- and co-regulation, I highly recommend Stuart Shanker's work.

For now, it's important to be clear that for educators to create a culture of agency, they need to view conflict as normal, necessary, and an opportunity for learning. Naming this loudly and proudly will help you gain the confidence to pause and give time to supporting children's agency in resolving their conflicts. It starts with the belief that young children are capable of solving problems themselves. The opposite would be to step in and resolve the issue yourself. Removing the red car doesn't help anyone have a way to work out that problem when it arises again in the future. It probably just escalates the feelings of injustice, and it will do nothing positive in building your relationships with the children involved.

https://self-reg.ca

Believing that children are capable of resolving conflict does not mean all children will have strategies for doing so or be at the same stage of social-emotional development. That is our job: to model and scaffold how to listen with respect, think of alternatives, and use strategies to self-regulate when feelings are big and overwhelming, as well as to make suggestions for children to try. I think this is one of the most important things we help young children navigate, and doing so is critical in those first few weeks of the school year.

Your Everyday Research

I wonder how much time and intention we give to supporting children to manage conflict. Reflect on the following questions to research your own context:

► Do I schedule so much into our day that there is no room to follow children and take opportunities to co-regulate conflict with them?

► Do I feel bad if I change the planned lesson to give children time to work through a disagreement?

► Do I unconsciously give children the message that they need an adult to solve problems for them, or do I project the belief that they are capable of working problems out themselves?

The Educator-Family Relationship

A child does not come to our setting alone. They are connected to a family and have relationships outside of preschool and school. In working with young children, we also work with families, so it follows that we should pay attention to family relationships in those important first weeks. The beginning of the year is so full and focused on the all-important child-educator relationship that sometimes we forget to make intentional plans for building relationships with families. Giving families time and attention now, however, will set up positive interactions and shared understandings for the rest of the school year.

When I was a primary school leader, we held a series of parent workshops before children started kindergarten/Foundation. Our intention was for parents to begin forming relationships, more so than using the forum to impart information about our school. We told families about uniforms, lunch orders, and specialist lessons in other ways. Instead, we focused the first session on exploring the question "What are your hopes and dreams for your child in their first year of school?" We sorted the families' responses on a wall to show how similar our hopes were. The largest groups of responses were always to be happy, to make friends, to enjoy school.

We can intentionally prioritize these hopes and dreams in what we make visible to families, particularly at the beginning of the year. You might use a digital platform to share the news of the day or speak in person with the families you see at the end of the day. No matter your form of communication, it is helpful as a team to be clear about what information you will prioritize in your sharing. Will you focus on their child knowing the colors of the rainbow, or talk about how they enjoyed building a block city, working on it for an extended time and developing friendships through their play? Keeping the hopes and dreams of the families in mind, it will be more powerful to share stories of friendship, growing confidence, and time when the child felt a sense of achievement. This is really what families want to know: is my child happy at school?

Families also want their children to be seen and known by the people at preschool or school. They want to feel that educators know their children, that we understand them. We can communicate how deeply we know the children by sharing things we know about their likes and interests or what is happening in their lives, showing we have taken the time to find out these things. We can show our sense of joy to families when we share stories of their children's learning or growth.

We can also create micro-moments of connection with families as well as children:

- Smile at the door as the family member drops off their crying child to child care, then send a follow-up text ten minutes later to say the child is now snuggled up with a soft toy, listening to a story.
- Chat for two minutes at the end of the day, asking how their day was or how the new baby is settling at home.
- Annotate photos or videos on the digital platform, documenting the child climbing a tree for the first time or sharing a joke with the class, to help the parent feel connected to life at school.

- Intentionally prioritize sharing moments of joy, curiosity, and engagement ahead of any concerns or struggles. This doesn't mean ignoring concerns but rather ensuring that a family hears about their competent, strong child as well.
- Share the words, tunes, and actions of songs and fingerplays you sing at preschool or school. Making a quick video of singing a favorite song helps families feel connected to school life and lets them sing it at home.
- Post videos of the learning spaces for family members who are unable to visit your site. This proved particularly important during times of COVID-19 restrictions.

Continuity of Relationships

It is very difficult to form secure and trusting relationships when the people you're trying to connect with keep changing. It seems like common sense, doesn't it? Yet so often we place young children in situations with fragmented relationships. In child care, they might have one educator for a couple of days and then one or more others because of the shift-work nature of the role. In primary schools, children are asked to navigate going to specialist teachers just as they are getting accustomed to their classroom teacher. I've even heard of this happening on their first day of school! It feels like pulling the rug out from under their feet to me.

What would it be like if, instead, we chose not to begin specialist lessons in the first week of primary school? I know this is a big wondering! I also know that it's tied to contract rights for educators to have preparation and noncontact time, but allow me to ask "what if" questions and see what thinking they might open for you.

- What if specialist teachers came into the classrooms, meeting the children where they are as they play and learn with their primary educators? In this way, specialist teachers are working to build connections and relationships with the children in the first few weeks, but they are not trying to teach the content of their subjects straightaway. After doing this for two weeks, the children will have greater confidence to transition back and forth from lessons.

- What if educators agreed to make up some of their preparation hours after the first couple of weeks of school? What if schools could organize a way to bank prep time so educators could take a day or half day to prep in a few weeks (and probably achieve more in that time)? Many schools in Australia are beginning to see the value and benefits of this system. It is more productive for educators, and it benefits children by allowing them the time to form strong and secure relationships when they most need it.

- What if preschool and child care educators worked within a primary caregiver model? In this model, each child is assigned to one educator who is principally responsible for caring for that child and communicating with their family. It does not mean exclusive care, and educators definitely interact with children outside their primary care group, but the model enables everyone to know who has primary responsibility for building a secure attachment with each child and fostering trust with their family. This happens quite naturally in family child care settings.

I don't have a solution to the shift-work nature of early childhood education and care settings, I'm afraid. This is too intertwined with the low value placed on the important work of early childhood educators and early education and care generally, as well as the low pay and demanding work conditions. If I had a magic wand, I would elevate the value and importance of early childhood educators in society and ensure they were remunerated for the specialized knowledge and expertise they have. With those improved conditions, perhaps more educators could stay in the field long-term, and we would have a chance of limiting the shift-work rotational nature of the work. But even working in our current system, I'm wondering:

- What if child care leaders prioritized continuity of relationships when scheduling shifts each month? It would be an improvement if children were able to stay with the same educator as much as possible, for two or three or four days in a row.

- What if children and educators stayed together over several years, rather than the common practice of moving children between rooms or groups as they age, while educators stay attached to a predetermined age range? Keeping an educator with the same group of children as they age can also happen in primary schools and allows connection and understanding to develop and deepen over time.

Continuity of Place

During those years when I had the honor of teaching five-year-olds, I remember something that happened at the start of every year, no matter the school I was teaching in. At least half of the children would play right on the class doorstep or outside the staff room door when it was recess, lunch, or playtime. Some children would venture off into the playground space within a few days, but it took weeks for others to feel confident in leaving the places where they felt secure.

I think they were staying close partly because of their attachment to me (since I was in the staff room having lunch or meeting with a colleague), but also because of their attachment to place. They had connected to our classroom space and felt they belonged there. Now they were locked out (literally) of the place that felt safe to them.

I would make some different choices if I were given a chance to relive this time. In Australian schools, teachers are rostered on several yard duties each week. These can be in any number of places where children are playing during recess and lunch breaks, often including the school library, gym, and hall spaces. This often stops educators from being able to be in the classroom during recess and lunch. I know many educators, particularly those teaching kindergarten/Foundation, who choose to stay in the classroom when they don't have a yard duty so that children can stay near them in the first weeks of school. But what if we made formal adjustments to support children better during this time?

- What if the teachers of young children, particularly children beginning school for the first time, were rostered for yard duty in spaces alongside the young children in their care? Instead of taking a turn supervising older children in the large and noisy school gym, they would remain assigned to the early years playground area for the first term of school.
- What if school leaders and specialists offered to do a little extra yard duty for the first two or three weeks of school so the kindergarten teachers could support children—without the extra responsibility of supervising other children's play— as they build connections to other play spaces in the school? This would give children time to develop connections to place before their teacher leaves them during playtime. Gradually, children learn to trust that their teacher will return after a while.

Relationships are everything. When we give time and energy to developing positive, open, and trusting relationships with children and families, we reap the rewards for the rest of the year. Any concern or uncertainty that arises is more likely to be resolved in a positive way because trust has been built. Children are more likely to thrive when they feel secure to be truly themselves. They will feel safe to be vulnerable, to take risks, to share their thinking and wonderings, and to use their agency to initiate their learning. Relationships are everything.

CHAPTER 3

Rituals of Belonging and Identity

In my everyday research for this book, I was fortunate to spend time in several preschools and schools, with some exceptional educators and lively, curious children. Each context was unique, but some patterns emerged in the learning spaces with the strongest cultures of agency. One of these patterns was the importance placed on rituals of belonging and identity. Each setting created and used different rituals, but each wove rituals into their days. Once I recognized this common thread, I started reading more about the role of ritual in our lives.

First we should clarify the difference between *ritual* and *routine*. Early childhood educators have long understood the value of routines in creating predictable and secure environments in which children can thrive. However, sometimes these routines become the driver of the day rather than a strategy for providing a predictable rhythm that is also flexible enough to follow the ebb and flow of children's play and emotions. I like to think of rituals as being routines with heart. Educators have chosen and developed these rituals for specific purposes, not just because they've always done things this way. Rituals move beyond the routine and are not rigid schedules to follow. They involve children; they are not something done to children. While they do connect to routines, rituals bring greater intentionality and deeper meaning to everyday events.

Linda Gillespie and Sandra Petersen (2012, 76) of Zero to Three expand on this idea:

> Rituals can be defined as special actions that help us navigate emotionally important events or transitions in our lives as well as enhance aspects of our daily routines to deepen our connections and relationships.

Each of the educators I observed created rituals for different purposes. Some rituals were for the pure joy of having fun together! At the same time, they served a higher purpose of building a sense of community, the feeling that we belong together. This sense of belonging is bigger than the individual. It's about the "we," the collective. The children and adults proclaim, "I belong because we belong together." Rituals help us feel connected to something bigger than ourselves and give meaning to the boundaries for living and learning together. Rituals act like superglue to bind individuals in a group. They're like the thread that runs through a set of beads on a necklace. Each bead remains beautiful and important in itself, but it is only when they are threaded together that the necklace shines and has real purpose.

Rituals That Build Group Identity

Some rituals help develop a sense that "we're in this together." They feel special to only this group: "If you're part of this group, then you'll know how this ritual goes." Sometimes these small moments of connection can appear unsophisticated or just some fun, but when we dig into them, we see how they bind people together. It's a way of proclaiming, "This is who we are, and this is what we value."

Your Everyday Research
Take a moment to think about your family or a special friendship group.
- What would you consider to be the rituals that proclaim your identity as a group of individuals who hold common values?
- Do you have a special farewell message as family members leave for work or school each morning?
- Do you have your own family rules for a favorite board game?
- Do you always greet certain friends with a kiss on the cheek, a fist bump, or a bear hug?

These are all rituals that build connection and belonging. When my niece Sienna was four, she would say, "See you later, alligator," and we would respond with, "In a while, crocodile." It was our farewell ritual that remained consistent for many years. One of my friendship groups has a ritual of creating an agenda before we begin our coffee and cake. Because we always have so much to share and our conversations can get very animated, we don't want to miss anything by talking over each other!

Rituals that build identity as a group include these:

- Greet each other in a different way each morning as you sit in a circle. A child chooses a different greeting each day, such as saying hello to the person on either side of you in a different language, using Auslan or American Sign Language to sign a morning greeting, or singing a greeting song together.

- Randomly choose a child's name from a basket so they can select which circle game, song, or fingerplay the group will do together.

- Sit in a circular shape to promote conversation and connection between children. Megan displays a sign in the classroom that proclaims, "Why do we sit in a circle? In the circle we are all equal. No one is behind you or in front of you. Everyone's thinking is important. The circle brings us together."

- Eat together, educators included. Liesl and her colleagues value this opportunity to sit with the children, outside and under the shade of a tree when possible, and enjoy this time of social connection.

- Create and say an Acknowledgment of Country each day. In Australia, this ritual is an important part of everyday life in educational settings. As professionals, we begin our meetings with a statement that acknowledges that we meet on the lands of First Nations peoples. In Adelaide, where I live, we live and work on Kaurna land. Like many preschools and schools in Australia, Angela's group begins each morning by proclaiming their Acknowledgment of Country. In Angela's group, seven-year-old Daisie wrote the statement for their group. Other settings sing or create movements to accompany their acknowledgment.

This is Daisie's Acknowledgment of Country, initiated by her after a visit from a guest Aboriginal musician who played his yidaki (didgeridoo):

I love everybody in the world.
We should respect Kaurna land and our ancestors.
We should never lie to people.
We should always be grateful to be on Kaurna land.
We should always respect our elders.

See videos of morning circle rituals with Angela's and Marcia's groups. At Ngutu College, each group begins the day with snack and a "yarning circle." The concept of a "yarning circle" comes from Australian First Nations culture and is a time of speaking and listening from the heart. It is a safe place to share feelings and ideas without judgment and provides the time for children to connect socially in an unhurried way each morning.

https://youtu.be
/T1qwqKJQtx8

Rituals That Support Transitions

No matter our age, transitions big and small can be challenging. Every day in every child care setting, preschool, and school, we ask children to make multiple transitions. Rituals support children in the transition from outdoors to indoors and between different learning experiences and times of the day. They help children transition, for example, from learning in the sandpit outdoors to learning with a story inside, or from independent reading time to sharing time. The rituals become predictable and stand as a marker of what is about to happen.

As adults, we have rituals to support our transitions too. Most of us have a bedtime ritual. It might include some yoga poses or reading a few pages of a novel. These rituals help us transition to sleep. As parents, you might use the bedtime ritual of reading two or three books to help young children move into sleep mode. I realized I have a ritual for when I arrive home from a day in a preschool or school. I take off my shoes, change into comfy clothes, and make a cup of coffee before hitting my email list at the computer. This ritual helps me transition into my home-working mode. I hope you're now thinking about the rituals that support your transitions.

The beginning and end of the day or session sets the tone for what happens next. Start-of-day rituals merit our attention because they support children to transition into sessions successfully. Rituals that mark the end of the day support children to transition from school to home. More than that, they provide children and educators an opportunity to pause and reflect on the day, building metacognitive awareness.

Megan begins each day with a "soft start," as we read in chapter 2. She then leads a consistent morning meeting that includes an Acknowledgment of Country, talking through the upcoming day, and noting any changes and special events for the day and the rest of the week. This ritual is very supportive of children, particularly any who feel anxious or unsure, helping them know what to expect of their day and their week. I imagine them taking a slow sigh and thinking, "Oh, it's okay now. I know what we're doing." In a similar way, the day ends with children (and Megan) sitting in a circle to share something from the day and, depending on the day and how much there is to share, reading aloud a picture book. Megan highlights any key things for the next day before the group joins in a farewell song or chant.

Kylie and Philomena, like many of their colleagues, place great value on their morning circle ritual. They acknowledge the land, say good morning in Kaurna (*Niina Marni*), and follow a ritual for checking in on how everyone is feeling. As children enter the classroom space, there is a tray of river stones labeled with each child's name. Each child places their stone in a box or basket to indicate how they're feeling as they arrive at school that morning. The feelings are indicated as a range, color coded with faces indicating emotions such as angry, nervous, excited, calm, hurt, upset, silly, and mad. All feelings are acknowledged. Children are taught that there aren't bad and good feelings. The educators say this practice helps them to identify who may benefit from some extra one-on-one time that day. Finally, the morning ritual always includes what the educators call a "positive primer," something that primes everyone in a positive way for the day, such as a game, song, or dance.

The three-, four-, and five-year-olds in Madlurta Wardli, the early childhood learning space at Ngutu College, begin their day choosing the area in which they want to learn, after which they have a long period of uninterrupted play and exploration. Some children choose to play inside while others move outdoors, and educators negotiate which adult will spend time in each area. They have two gathering times each day when children are called together. Each day, a different child is responsible for gathering everyone, choosing to sound a temple gong or a heart chime. Liesl says, "These whole-group intentional teaching times lead into lunch and home time so that the day's learning, in particular children's agency in their learning, is minimally interrupted."

Other rituals that support transitions include these:

- Visual timetables or schedules. These visual aids have become very common in Australian primary schools. They support children with a predictable environment. However, they only become a ritual when intentionality and participation are attached. If the visual timetable remains on the wall, it risks becoming mere decoration. Reading the flow of the day is part of Megan's morning meeting, during which children ask questions about each time of the day, clarifying their understandings, checking what will happen during that time. This happens in a natural and authentic way. It is not rushed. Megan doesn't announce, "Now it's time for questions," but she responds as a question naturally arises, as we would in conversations with our friends and colleagues. It feels authentic, fluid, and conversational. Megan understands that children have the right to participate in setting up their day. She often explains the reasons behind decisions for the flow and any changes to the usual pattern so children understand and feel included in the decision-making. There are times when the flow can be modified based on children's ideas, and other times when it cannot. But children are included in the thinking about it, not just told, "This is the way it is."
- Cleanup or pack-up time. Cleaning up often signals a transition, leaving the familiar experience to move into the new one. When we talk with children about the purpose of this time, we shift it from routine to ritual. The purpose is to reset the environment for the next learners or the next

time you want to play and engage with the materials. We're getting the environment ready for the next learning. My team intentionally uses the language "reset the learning environment" over "clean up" or "pack up." This subtle change in language also communicates that there will be an opportunity to return to the experience. "Clean up" feels more like something permanent, that the chance to revisit might be lost. Megan uses the words "Time to press Pause now, please." Her words communicate that learning is continuous, and that you'll have an opportunity to return to this at some time if you want or need to.

- Singing a song or playing music. Music can initiate the time to transition. Music also provides time for transitioning, rather than expecting it to happen immediately. Henry sings a circle song to gather the five-year-old learners together after some play and exploration. His colleague Erin sings as children reset their materials, gently coaxing children to come to the meeting area with the song. Other teachers play music while children dance to their meeting area. There is no need to say, "We're waiting for you," or "Show me you're ready," because everyone participates in the shared ritual of singing and moving, ready when the song is finished. And if everyone is not ready then? Sing another song!

See video of using song as a transition ritual in Henry's and Erin's classes.

https://youtu.be
/BBsNggeU12o

Rituals That Celebrate Each Other

My work takes me to many preschools and schools, and I often collaborate with educators on language and literacy learning. One day, as I was observing Jason as he worked with young authors, we gathered in the meeting area to "publish," or share, some of the most recent books the children had made. After the first child had read his book to the class, Jason quietly suggested a "rainfall congratulations." I had no idea what this was! The children clapped over their heads three times and let their fingers fall to the ground like water falling down a waterfall. I soon learned that the class had several special ways to congratulate each other for strong learning, including a "fireworks clap," a "round-about clap," and even a "woo-hoo double-air high-five"!

It was joyful and fun. It brought playfulness to their learning. It was also a ritual that proclaimed identity and belonging. Not being a member of this group, I didn't know their ritual, but I was soon welcomed into it—it wasn't exclusive or excluding.

Birthday rituals may also be important to your community, and they do not always have to involve cake and candles. We can bring meaning and intentionality to how we celebrate this special day in other ways. I remind myself that birthday rituals are to celebrate the birth of that person, to take joy in the fact their birth happened, and to feel happy that they are with us.

Some birthday rituals beyond cake and candles include these:

- Invite a small group of children to prepare a birthday tray for the birthday child by selecting some items that are important to the birthday child. For example, children select a toy car for Toby because he loves to name different cars in the parking lot. They give Charlie a toy lion because he loves *The Lion King* so much. Isabella's tray includes a toy unicorn, and Jada's has fancy pencils because she loves to draw. The children add a small vase with a flower, twig of rosemary, herbs, or leaves from the preschool garden and perhaps a special glass for a drink of water. Finally, they choose a picture book the birthday child would enjoy. The group sings "Happy Birthday" and claps the child's age, the educator reads the book out loud, and everyone enjoys a cool drink together.
- Make a birthday book for the birthday child. Each child contributes a page that names something special about the birthday child. One example I saw included pages that read, "Jada is good at drawing," "Jada has curly hair," and "I like to play in the sandpit with Jada."

- Have a special, silly birthday ritual no one else does. When I was a new teacher, my first principal, Mike Veal, introduced this ritual for all birthdays, whether you were a child or adult. I have no idea where it came from, and perhaps Mike made it up! The birthday person was invited to stand on a stool or platform. Following the singing of "Happy Birthday," the birthday person either clucked like a hen or crowed like a rooster! Everyone roared with laughter and clapped and cheered joyously. I clearly remember doing this in front of the school (we had only fifty-two children) when I turned twenty-one. This might not be the ritual you would choose, but perhaps you can think of something equally as silly and fun for your community. You would never want to embarrass the birthday person, so you can create a set of three or four different ideas with the children at the beginning of the year, providing some choice for the birthday child.

At the same time, we as educators must be mindful that birthdays are not celebrated in all religions and cultures. In this case, we need to navigate birthday rituals carefully so as not to unintentionally cause a child to feel excluded. Remember that this is all about creating a sense of belonging. Imagine for a moment the perspective of a child who does not celebrate birthdays in their family culture. Perhaps they are the only one in their class or group who doesn't have a birthday party, but to them it can feel as if every week another child is celebrated in this special way at school or preschool. How isolating it could be for them if the birthday ritual was a large focus. In these situations, it's wise to take a light touch when making birthdays a focus. You might not need to ignore them completely, but perhaps birthdays are celebrated within a small group rather than with the whole class or large group.

I hope these rituals spark some ideas for you to try. Perhaps you value other rituals that I've not mentioned. I hope this chapter affirms their importance and brings meaning and intentionality to each of them. Instead of just doing them because you always have, think about the deeper meaning and purpose behind them.

How Do Rituals Support a Culture of Agency?

Agency is a deeply held feeling and also an action. Emotion and action are intricately entwined. To take action within a group, you need to feel safe to do so. In the learning environments I researched, children certainly seemed to feel secure and safe. They seemed to feel that they were the owners of their learning and their lives. They also acted. They initiated their learning. This is at the heart of agency.

Feeling that you belong and that you are seen, known, and celebrated for who you are is very empowering. You know it's safe to take risks and make mistakes. You know that because the community members understand and value you, they will pick you up and support you if you stumble. As the saying goes, they'll always "have your back." The freedom to be and to do emerges from your sense of belonging and identity.

Rituals create community. They create a togetherness that brings about the confidence to be ourselves. This confidence enables us to try new experiences and to share our ideas and feelings without the fear of being embarrassed. The community holds you in a nest of security, allowing you to explore, experiment, and adventure—to use your agency. The stronger the nest, the more secure each person feels and the more agentive they are in their learning.

CHAPTER 4

The Language of Agency

The old saying goes, "Sticks and stones may break my bones, but names will never hurt me." We used to think this was helpful self-talk to build resilience, but the truth is, words *can* and *do* hurt. They also reveal our values, beliefs, and, in the case of an educator, the way we view the child. One of the most important, if not *the* most important, tool in our educator tool kit is our language. The words we choose, the tone we use, and our nonverbal language convey strong messages to children, families, and our colleagues. Language has the power to build up—or take down.

You will recall that we touched on our image of the child in chapter 1, when we considered the importance of sharing power with children. The words we use in our interactions with children also reveal if we unconsciously see them as

- innocents, needing our protection;
- threatening to our feeling of being in control;
- empty, ready to be filled up with knowledge; or
- capable of initiating and guiding their own learning by thinking, feeling, and theorizing.

Take a moment to imagine the following scene: A group of four-year-old children and their educators are at their local national park, enjoying a day of learning and exploring in nature (regularly called "bush-kindy" in Australia). This is something they do regularly, not a one-off field trip or excursion, so children have developed an attachment to place and a feeling of familiarity. Children are playing and exploring in various ways. Several are collecting branches to build a fort. Others are persisting in attempts to tie branches together with twine as an educator holds them in place. One pair have found a quiet place under a tree where they are mixing potions. Five children and an educator are gathered around some fallen logs, using magnifying glasses to observe the ants busy at work.

Suddenly, the fort builders explode with noise, arguing about the building process. They run through the group of potion makers and ant researchers with their sticks in the air. How might an educator respond?

- Response A: "That group, get back to work on your forts! This isn't a time for running around."
- Response B: "Stop running with those sticks! You'll hurt someone!"
- Response C: "When you're loud and running around like that, it stops the other groups from learning, and I find it hard to hear the children I'm listening to here."
- Response D: "What's going on, everyone? Remember how you collaborated to build a fort yesterday? I know you can work it out. What could you do to work it out today?"

Each of these responses conveys different beliefs about learning and the educator's image of the child.

Response A conveys that learning is a chore and the children are doing a task. It reveals how the teacher believes they are the boss and holds an image of children as needing to be controlled. The educator might be feeling threatened by the loud and boisterous arguing of the children, as if they may soon lose or already have lost control of the situation.

Response B primarily shows a concern for safety. It reveals an idea that children are not capable of being responsible or that children need an adult's protection because they can't be trusted to play with sticks safely.

Response C speaks to the belief that learning happens in a social context, where the rights of others are respected. The words communicate to children that they have a responsibility to others.

Response D reveals an image of competent children who can collaborate and solve their own social problems. "Remember how you collaborated to build a fort yesterday? I know you can work it out" communicates a belief in their ability to think and act. They can be trusted. They have the skills and intelligence. The words convey an unspoken message too: "I know you've got this."

Intentional Teaching

Detailed in his 1990 book *Life in Classrooms*, researcher Philip Jackson found that educators make about fifteen hundred decisions each day! No wonder you often go home tired—you have decision fatigue, meaning your brain is so exhausted and overloaded that it cannot effectively do more complex thinking (Jackson 1990). Decision overload happens because, at its best, teaching is a very intentional role. The efforts in teaching are not random or routine. Everything, including the words we use, can be intentionally chosen to create opportunities for learning.

In Australia the term *intentional teaching* is becoming widely used. I find it both helpful and reassuring. The Australian curriculum guide for children aged birth to five, *Belonging, Being, and Becoming: The Early Years Learning Framework for Australia* (Council of Australian Governments 2009, 17), defines it as this:

> Intentional teaching involves educators being deliberate, purposeful and thoughtful in their decisions and actions. Intentional teaching is the opposite of teaching by rote or continuing with traditions simply because things have always been done this way.

At times children's learning benefits from explicit teaching, such as when we want to demonstrate how to safely use a hot glue gun. At other times, it is wise to be less explicit so that we leave room for children's curiosity, theorizing, and thinking. Even when the context calls for less explicit teaching (that is, less demonstration or direct instruction), it does not mean we are less intentional in our teaching decisions. Every one of those fifteen hundred decisions is, potentially, the opportunity to be intentional and consider what is best for children's learning and well-being.

So much informs our intentionality as educators:

- our knowledge of child development
- our understanding of learning theory
- our knowledge of each child and their family
- our observations of the child in interaction with other children
- our curriculum goals

Being deliberate and purposeful in using the language of agency comes from our desire for children to have the skills and strategies to initiate and lead their own learning. It comes from wanting children to see themselves as powerful and competent learners. And so, it means educators do not unnecessarily rescue children from their struggles. When a child can't zip up their rain coat or the roof of their block construction continues to collapse, we can pause and bring agentive intentions to the words we use to respond. "Let me help you with that," might be said with good intentions and offer a quick way out of the struggle, but it will not support the child in devising a strategy to use the next time they encounter a struggle.

In my everyday research, a very strong pattern was evident in all the settings I observed, whether I was watching Mimi with three- and four-year-olds or Kylie and Philomena with eight-year-olds. The words they chose communicated a belief in the capacity of the child to be an active problem solver. All the educators were intentional in using language that helped children understand the importance of persistence and flexible thinking when learning.

I heard language such as this:

- "I can see you're a bit stuck. What are you going to try next?"
- "You look as if you're a bit stuck. Can you see something that might help close by?"
- "What could you do about that, do you think?"
- "What have you tried already? Why do you think that didn't work?"
- "I can see you're not giving up on that. You're persisting and trying different ways to figure it out."
- "You'll get there! I can see you're not giving up."
- "I can see people gathering some evidence to support their thinking."

Let's dig into the intentional thinking behind these words.

Praise versus Encouragement

Everyone likes a bit of praise. It makes us feel good. It's just not very helpful in creating the kind of learning culture we're interested in. At its worst, praise can create a dependency, like any reward system. Children can become dependent on getting praise from an adult. They begin to see value in their learning only when it has been validated by an adult and not for any intrinsic satisfaction it might bring.

I can tell a lot about a learning culture when I visit a learning setting, whether it be a primary classroom, the mud patch in a preschool, or bush-kindy. If children frequently seek an adult's praise with questions such as, "Do you like my potion/painting/pattern?" it tells me that they are used to being validated with some version of, "Yes! I love it," or "Yes! It's beautiful," no matter the effort that has been applied. These children seem to create their learning only so that the teacher can give it a big tick of approval. And they waste time by seeking an adult's praise when they could be engaged in exploration.

We need to be careful not to create a culture of learning where children believe they need to show everything to an adult for it to be worthy. Instead, our words and actions need to intentionally show children that the endeavor of learning is satisfying in itself, struggles and all. The agentive learning culture envelopes children in ways of being that make their own evaluation and sense of satisfaction important. So, the next time a child shows you something they have achieved or created, instead of praising it with, "I love it!" or "Well done!" try one of the suggestions on page 48.

Less of . . .
• "Great job!"
• "Well done!"
• "I like your . . ."
• "I love it when you . . ."
• "Wow! That's beautiful."

More of . . .
• "Tell me more about this."
• "I can see that you . . ."
• "I noticed that . . ."
• "Hmm . . ." (And smile.)
• "You look proud. Are you? What are you proud about?"
• "I'm so curious. How did you do that?"
• "You look [happy, proud, excited]. It feels good to [swing high, climb the tree]."
• "When you keep trying new things, it gives you more ideas about what you like to do."
• "What was the hardest [or easiest] part?"
• "Would you show me and Jessie (another child) how you made that?"
• "Hmm . . . I wonder what you'll come up with next."
• "You did it!"
• "Ooh, what did you learn from that?" (With a curious tone.)
• "How did you come up with that idea?"

Brave Learners

In the learning settings I visited, I noticed that educators emphasized opportunities for children to stretch themselves physically and intellectually. We'll talk more about the intellectual challenges in chapter 6. For now, let's look at the value of physical challenges.

All the educators provided opportunities for children to climb, scramble, crawl, tie, place, jump, balance, and roll in authentic and engaging contexts and for different purposes. Encountering physical challenges stretches children and helps them develop the confidence to try new things. It helps children imagine they are someone who *can*. However, watching children struggle with something physical can sometimes lead adults to fear the worst: that they will be hurt. The image of the innocent child takes over our brains!

I remember watching my five-year-old niece, Quinn, climb higher and higher up a tree that was unfamiliar to her. My internal conversation went something like this, "Will she be okay? Yes, I think she'll know when to stop. But what if she doesn't? Should I step in? Am I overreacting? If I step in, will I stop her from using her agency? Will she stop believing she can do it? I think she's got it—it will be okay." It was so difficult to know what I should do!

So, what words could we use in this situation (and others where we feel a little nervous about the safety of the children)? Often the first thing that comes to mind is, "Be careful!" But that's probably not the best choice. "Be careful!" doesn't support children to build self-awareness. If they always hear these words, the danger is they'll begin to monitor their decisions only when given this cue. We want children to be constantly aware and to self-monitor their actions and decisions when involved in something that challenges them, not reliant on a cue from an adult.

Here are some other suggestions:

- "Stay focused on what you're doing. You're doing well."
- "I can see you're taking your time and not rushing."
- "Do you feel [stable, secure, safe, strong] on that [rock, branch]?"
- "How are you feeling?"

- "I noticed how safely you picked up the saw, so I know you'll be using it safely too."
- "Remember that sticks need space. Look around you. Do you have enough space to swing that big stick?"
- "Ask him if he's still having fun."
- "Check in with your friends to see if that's okay with them."

Learning to Learn

I often think of the famous saying "Give a man a fish and you feed him for a day; teach a man to fish and you feed him for a lifetime." A culture of agency is a lot like this. Educators are interested in helping children learn to learn, not merely to memorize facts and develop isolated skills. The teachers I spent time with used intentional language to instill in children the notion that they were learners. They made the learning process visible with their words.

Educators who want to support children's agency notice and name ideas and strategies that are helpful to learning. They intentionally model this practice and (here's the explicit teaching part) name what they notice so that this learning process, this way of thinking, becomes visible to the children.

"I noticed that you chose to use big and bold writing for that word, Sahil. Can you please explain to us why you did that?" asks Danni.

"I'm noticing how well your group is collaborating to reset your area," Kylie says to a group as they reset an area where they have been exploring probability with a set of wooden bowling pins.

"I saw how you carried that bucket of water all the way to the sandpit all by yourself, Alice. You're such an independent learner!" proclaims Mimi.

The educators' words show children that, by acting strategically, they can achieve and accomplish things. They show children that they are the kinds of learners who have achievements. They can make it happen. They have agency.

This intentional teaching sets up children to successfully notice themselves. It supports the development of self-efficacy. It grows metacognitive awareness: the ability to think about our thinking and learning processes. Metacognition includes reflecting on successes and struggles, revising plans along the way, and planning ahead for what we might need. When learning is nudged to the metacognitive level, the child not only engages successfully in learning but also is aware of the strategies they used and decision-making they undertook. Of course, metacognition also has a developmental aspect, but instead of seeing a child as too young or not capable of metacognition, I prefer to see them as holding the potential for this sophisticated thinking. This view opens possibilities for me to help children to notice and name what they are doing, knowing I am supporting their metacognitive awareness to develop.

The more an educator notices and names something, the more the child will also see it and the more chance there is for that process to be internalized. Then the knowledge or strategy can be used in different contexts. By naming the child's learning strategies rather than just praising them, we give children the words to hang the idea or concept on. So, when Alice decides she wants water in the sandpit and proceeds to get the bucket, fill it up, and carry it to the river she's creating, Mimi names her as "an independent learner." It becomes something Alice knows she can be and something she can now call on when learning next. Maybe next time, it won't be water she needs but a certain color paint or a different-sized crate for her loose parts construction.

Numerous times, I heard the educators ask children, "What do you notice?" The children are ready for this question because the educator has always modeled their own noticing. What is most critical when asking this question, though, is that the children trust that their teacher is interested in their ideas, not just searching for right answers. They trust that their teacher will accept their responses and their emerging theories and ideas. Trust builds security. When an educator asks children to share what they notice, it comes from an interest in multiple possibilities, not from a goal to find one specific response (what I call "guess what's in the teacher's head" questions). Very soon this becomes the norm: this is what you do to learn. You look closely, you notice details and patterns, you share them, and you think about them together. There is agency in learning how to learn, and noticing and naming is one tool in the children's learning tool kit.

The educators I observed also gave considerable space for enhancing metacognitive awareness. They made time to pause and plan or reflect on the learning processes. This sometimes happened in circle times, mini-lessons, or reflection and share times. It sometimes happened in the moment, side by side with children as they made a book or created a pirate ship from loose parts. The one thing in common was a focus on the learning process over the end product. It's not like the teachers ignored the book or pirate ship, but their questions were more interested in highlighting the children's learning processes, their thinking. I jotted the following questions in my notebook over several site visits:

- What kinds of thinking might help us with this learning?
- What is your plan?
- What materials do you think you'll need?
- How did you figure that out?
- What made you change your mind?
- That's so interesting. Why did you choose that material?
- Did you get stuck anywhere? How did you get unstuck?

When Times Get Tough

As we explored earlier, conflict is a natural part of life. While we don't wish the big conflicts on anyone, accepting that conflict will happen helps us prepare our response to it. Let's consider two possible sources of conflict in an early learning setting: interpersonal conflict and intellectual conflict.

Interpersonal conflict tends to be up front and in your face. Jordan and Miki fight over the most favored doll in the home-play area. Sahil feels excluded from the game the other children are playing at lunchtime. Rosie feels angry that Morgan doesn't follow the rules of the game they've created. Interpersonal conflict happens every day in every early learning setting.

How we respond to interpersonal conflict reveals how we view the child. Do we see that children are capable of resolving conflicts, or do we believe they can't do it, so we need to resolve it for them? Of course, we often need to model, scaffold, and support children in their conflict resolution. This isn't a "just let them be" approach. But we can see conflict as an opportunity to learn and practice strategies, not as something we need to resolve for children as quickly as possible.

The language we choose to use in these situations is powerful. It begins with listening and taking the children's feelings seriously. Then what we say can support them in self-regulating and learning to work things out. Let's look at some examples I collected in my research and reflect on the values and view of the child they embody:

"It looks as if you're feeling pretty upset at the moment. Let's have a drink of water and find a place where we can talk through it together."	• Recognizes, validates, and names the child's feelings. • Suggests a strategy for self-regulation. • Provides support to co-regulate.
"What have you already tried?" followed by "Why do you think that didn't work?"	• Tells the child, "I believe you are someone who has strategies and is capable of resolving this. I know you would have tried some things." • Some children may be too upset to reflect on the second question. You can return to it later, once the big emotions have subsided.
"Let's name some options. What could you do to work this out together?"	• There are options; there is not just one way to fix this. • This question provides an opportunity for the educator to name some strategies that the children may not have thought of yet. This is supportive co-regulation. • Remember, in the heat of the moment, children may not be able to think through these and will benefit from some time to self-regulate first.

The words that the educators I observed chose were one of their most powerful tools for supporting children's agency. The words flowed naturally from them, which showed me they use them all the time. This is how culture is built too. When children hear words that support them to make decisions, take action, determine their next steps, and initiate learning, they start to see themselves as learners who do these things. Hearing them once or twice is not enough, but hearing them daily, over time, addressed to many different children, and in different contexts builds a culture so children expect to learn this way. Children imagine themselves as learners who *can* because their teacher believes they can. This belief turns to action, the self-efficacy we read about in chapter 1.

I think it's helpful to share some words from my research notebook. Language evolves over time, and being more intentional with our words takes effort. As my friend and colleague Matt Glover says, we all need to go to "language rehab" for something! I find it helpful to see these words and to read them out loud so they form in my mouth as well as in my mind. I might take one or two intentions with me for a week or so, practicing and using these words until they become part of my repertoire as an educator. Here are some of the powerful words I heard when visiting the settings, particularly when educators were supporting children to self-regulate or participate:

- "If you need to move your body to see and hear, please do that now."
- "Can you share that thinking in a minute? We'll just hear from Connor first."
- "Amal and Lola, I can see you're having a chat about this too. It would be great if you'd share your thinking with us all in a minute."
- "It looks as if you would like to [play with the cars too]. How can I help you be able to join in?"

Intellectual conflict also happens every day in early learning settings. It happens a lot more in agentive cultures than in compliant cultures. All members of an agentive culture expect and accept that struggles are a natural part of learning and that everyone, young and old, will experience it. Struggles are seen as an opportunity to learn, grow, and stretch. They are celebrated for offering moments of resilience, problem solving, and flexible thinking. Learning is not always easy and straightforward. If it is, you're probably not stretching yourself but instead are stuck in a pattern of practicing what you already know. Whether we are three or thirty-three, we all need some "wonderful uneasiness" to fully engage in learning in our zones of proximal development. It is important that, as educators, we do not unintentionally give children the message that to be successful learners, they must find learning easy. The Learning Zones diagram explored in chapter 1 could be helpful here.

The way educators responded to children's learning struggles emerged as another strong pattern in my everyday research. Above all, they expected and wanted learning struggles to happen. The learning contexts they created enabled children to experience intellectual conflict (more about this in chapter 6). When a child got stuck in their learning, educators would respond with words such as these:

- "Have you seen someone else try something that worked for them?"
- "What if you pretended you could do it? What would that look like?"
- "Who do you think could help you with this?" (Encourage them to name another child, not the educator.)
- "When this happens to me, I sometimes [offer a strategy], so you might want to try that and see if it works for you."

Nonverbal Language

Language is also nonverbal. Our body language communicates tone and intent. As educators, we all know the power of a sideways look, which we might give a child who is considering something not so safe or appropriate. There are highly qualified people who can teach you about nonverbal gestures and body language. I learned so much from my Deaf friends when I was learning American Sign Language during my time in New York. Instead, I want to explore a pedagogical strategy that is nonverbal but creates an opportunity for talking—that is, considering when to ask children to raise their hands to have a turn to speak and when not to.

Overwhelmingly, the educators in my everyday research asked for children to raise their hands sparingly, and no hand raising to speak in a group was their default. This intentional decision had a great impact on the climate, tone, and culture of their learning communities. When I suggest no hand raising to educators, the most common response is fear that things will get out of hand, and perhaps that the teacher will lose control. So, let's dig into this a little to help us understand why not always requiring children to raise their hands to speak is important for children's agency in learning.

Meet Layla. She's representing many children in our preschools and schools. Layla has just turned five and begun primary school. She loves school, just as she loved going to kindy when she was four. School is different from kindy, though. You can't go outside to play when you want to, for starters. You have to ask the teacher if you can go to the toilet, even if you're really bursting. And there are big kids at school, but Layla keeps away from them on the playground, so it's okay.

Layla has learned a lot about school already. In her very first week, maybe even on the first day, she learned the most important lesson: "When you have something to say, you put your hand up." Well, that's not exactly true, because one time Layla really wanted to tell her teacher that her puppy made a mess in the house before she came to school and that her dad got mad. But when she put her hand up, her teacher didn't ask her to talk. And that's the next rule: "Don't talk unless the teacher calls your name."

The next thing Layla learned about class discussions was that you have to wait for the teacher to ask a question and then put your hand up, but only if your idea is the same one the teacher wants. Soon Layla realized that Brayden and Jaysean and Lucy always put their hands up and that the teacher almost always asks them what they think. So, Layla figured she didn't have to put her hand up because Brayden and Jaysean and Lucy will do that, and the teacher will be happy.

What is concerning in this story—for all the Laylas in our settings—is that when you learn that you don't have to put your hand up because the teacher will always ask someone else, you don't get involved in the conversation. It leads to nonparticipation in learning. But more worrying, it takes just a little step to go from "I don't have to put my hand up" to "I don't have to think because I won't be called to share my thinking anyway."

I have a theory that we have a lot of "pretend learners" in our classrooms. These are children like Layla who like school and want to please the teacher. They are compliant but not engaged. This is very dangerous. If our primary goal in education is learning, and many children are pretending to be learning, then we need to do something about it.

Amanda shares her experience:

At first I used pop sticks (wooden craft sticks) with names on them, which were placed in a cup. Instead of waiting or asking for learners to put their hands up to answer a question, volunteer for a task, or express an opinion, I would state the question or task and then select a stick to determine who would answer, talk, or get the job. This led to some anxiety, glee, and mathematical reasoning about the likelihood of names being drawn out. At first it was fun, but then some reactions began to emerge.

Prior to the No Hands Up rule, Leticia and David had monopolized the answering of questions and always had their hands up. After the new rule, Leticia got quite angry and stated, "It's not fair," several times over the first couple of weeks. David became exasperated when other learners did not know the answers and he did. A few of the learners who had previously hidden themselves away became quite anxious and responded consistently with "I don't know." I accepted "I don't know" as an answer but then asked them to find out (various strategies were accepted for this, including asking a friend). As everyone realized the system was not going to go away, and that they all had equal chances of being chosen each time, there were fewer negative reactions and "I don't know" responses and, in my observations, more engagement with the question or topic.

I learned two big things about my own practice. One was that the pop stick name strategy made me pause. I realized that when I required hands up to speak, I would launch straight into selecting a child to respond. There was no thinking time. Reaching for the stick jar was a good visual prompt for everyone to have some thinking time and to mentally prepare a response.

Second, I learned that I really did ignore some children a lot more than others. This strategy engaged me in children's responses as much as it did them. I became keen to see who would be chosen and hear what they would say. Because everyone had a response prepared, and there was some disappointment in not being chosen, I often gave children opportunities to share their thinking with a friend. For this reason, I began using miniature whiteboards as a group-time strategy for children to record their ideas (in words or sketches). This way, all thinking is recorded and shared more often, rather than hearing only from those who offered it by raising their hands.

I have continued with the No Hands Up strategy since that year. I believe it encourages high levels of engagement and involvement. It provides opportunities for children to practice thinking, responding, and then sharing in a public forum. Even four weeks of this practice made me a better group leader, and I became more reflective of my questioning and thinking-out-loud techniques.

Participation is essential in the agentive culture. Using a No Hands Up strategy—whether Turn and Talk (also known as Think-Pair-Share), pop-stick names, or others—increases participation. I often use another strategy that I call "Teacher Voice Off." I explain to the children that I will not be choosing whose turn it is to talk. They'll listen for a gap in the conversation, just as regular conversations happen, and then share their thinking. I'll often say, "Sometimes two or more people will start talking at the same time, but I know that you'll work it out if it happens so that we get to hear everyone's thinking." I find that explicitly stating that we'll use the Teacher Voice Off strategy particularly helps children who are accustomed to the teacher deciding who is called on to share, because they know the only thing that is expected of them is to participate. At first we practice using the Teacher Voice Off strategy with low-risk topics, like sharing ideas about a favorite game or sharing thinking about a picture book I just read aloud to them. Later we'll move on to conversations that involve deeper thinking and differing perspectives. I'll often first suggest rehearsing by turning and talking to their partners to build everyone's confidence to participate. I purposefully do not talk, but instead I model active listening as the conversation moves between children. It feels so different from the traditional question-and-answer mode of teaching, as if we are growing our thinking together.

See video of Marcia's yarning circle (morning ritual) for an example of a No Hands Up conversation.

https://youtu.be
/vlEtB1knPW0

When we ensure the questions we pose are not "guess what's in the teacher's head" questions but are worthy of thinking and talking about, we create the conditions for children to participate. When we enter into the conversation with genuine interest in a child's thinking, we are less likely to ask a question that is closed and seeks a right answer. Instead of wanting to find out if a child remembers the name of the character from the read-aloud, we are interested in what kind of a person they think the character is, and why. Often the most open question is the best: "What are you thinking?" followed by "What makes you think that?" asked with genuine curiosity. When "What are you thinking?" becomes our default, children learn that we are interested in their ideas. They learn that it is safe to share their thinking and that it will be accepted and respected.

CHAPTER 5

The Environment for Agency

As I read through my notebooks and looked at the photographs of the diverse learning spaces I visited, a quotation widely attributed to Maya Angelou came to mind: "Every person needs a place that is furnished with hope." This statement sums up how the educators thought about the physical, temporal, and emotional environments they intentionally created for children. When I drew together my observations and the many hours spent engaging with children in these spaces, I realized they are all places "furnished with hope."

Hope is a feeling of expectation and desire. I hope it won't rain when we have our picnic tomorrow. I hope I find just the right story for this chapter. I hope that every child discovers the joy of reading.

I find the history and origins of English words fascinating, so I also researched the etymology of *hope*. Historically, hope was connected to the word and the meaning of *trust*, as in, "I trust your mother is feeling better." Doesn't that sound like the learning communities we've been exploring together? They are places of *hope* and *trust*.

Children in agentive cultures learn to trust the environment, the adults, and each other. They come to school with the hope—the expectation—that educators will give time to the questions they are curious about and interested in. They come with hope that this space and these relationships will support them to grow and learn. Hope is optimistic and filled with potential, not limitation. Their hope isn't unfounded but given wings.

The children who are part of Angela's, Mimi's, and Katie's communities come to preschool or school with ideas about what they want to explore and learn. Time and time again, I've witnessed children arrive in the morning, proclaiming, "I've been thinking about [an inquiry focus or math concept or art creation], and I know what I'm going to do today." Or "I already know what my next book will be about!" Conversely, compliant cultures do not support children to initiate their learning, nor do they honor children's agency. Children in these learning cultures learn to come to school or preschool and wait for the teacher to tell them what to do. These compliant cultures create dependency.

The educators in agentive cultures are filled with hope and optimism too. They see children through this lens. They hope for each child to engage deeply with learning and to build relationships that enrich their lives. More than carrying a wishful hope, the educators *trust* children will do so when given the best environment for learner agency.

So, that's the big picture: our hope-filled, trust-filled vision for the learning spaces that will support children to thrive. But how do we get there? What requires our intentionality when we are creating agentive learning environments?

I prefer to understand people as being an integral part of the environment, rather than as something separate or something that is merely entering the environment. Our relationships with space and place are much deeper and more beautifully intertwined than that. As we've already spent considerable time exploring relationships and intentional language, which helps us understand the emotional environment, this chapter will focus on the temporal and physical environments.

The Temporal Environment

Time is part of the environment. Educators interested in creating an agentive culture are intentional about the way time is used. In deciding the daily flow or schedule, they ask themselves these questions:

- How do we want the flow of time to feel for children and educators?
- What experiences will we ensure we make time for?
- What experiences will we not give as much time to in the day or week?
- How will we transition with children between different learning experiences and different times of the day?

They also ponder questions like, "How much time will we give to children for each learning experience?" and "What will be the sequence, rhythm, and flow of the day?" It is particularly important to think seriously about these questions at the beginning of the school year, but it's valuable to reflect on them at any time of the year. It's never too late to do some tweaking. After all, that's the "wonderful uneasiness" of growth: to be continually reflecting and revising.

One intentional decision about time stood out in my everyday research. *Every* educator I observed began the day with some flexible time, like Megan's "soft start." This time was often longer at the beginning of the year, as teachers used it to engage with children, learn about them, and build those all-important relationships. For example, Ngutu College in Adelaide begins each day with forty-five minutes of "community time"—a time of self-directed and self-selected playing indoors and outdoors—for the entire community of students, from preschool to Year 9.

The educators I researched also tended to chunk the days into longer periods of exploration, play, and learning, whether in a preschool or primary school setting. Some primary classes flowed from a reading workshop to a writing workshop to a word study. Others flowed from mathematics explorations to read-alouds to inquiry projects. Some preschools held small-group circle times before a long, uninterrupted playtime. Others held their small-group circle times later in the day. The schedules (or flow of the day) were not cookie-cutter models of each other by any means. What they had in common was an intention to give long, uninterrupted times for learning, rather than break up the day into small (sometimes disconnected) periods of time, allowing for flexibility in the rhythm of the day. When children are particularly engaged in their play one morning, it's easy to allow it to continue for fifteen extra minutes. When children are focused and engrossed in their small-group inquiry projects, the time can be extended and the read-aloud moved to after lunchtime or even the next day.

Some primary teachers also experimented with half-day or whole-day explorations so children had time to dive deeply into their learning. This worked particularly well once children had settled into the year and had begun some independently led learning projects (like in a writing workshop and inquiry project work).

One year Amanda worked with a group of committed six- and seven-year-old writers. They had developed strong identities as authors, so much so that when the timer would signal that independent writing time was coming to an end for the day, Amanda would regularly be met with groans and "Why can't we write for longer?" Amanda joked, "I think you would write *all* day if you could!" A few weeks passed, and the opportunity came for Amanda to respond to the children's pleas. She proposed a Writer's Retreat Day and asked the class what they thought. "Yes!" was the unanimous cry. Together they planned the day: a whole day for working on their books, ensuring they would be ready for an upcoming book launch. The day had some structure, predictability, and flow to it: recess and lunchtime, two share circles, a nature walk to get oxygen for their creative brains, and a video of Mo Willems talking about his writing process for inspiration. But most of the day, the children and Amanda had long stretches of time to make books and confer about them. They also had stations set up for snacks, hand massages, and mentor text inspiration, and a "Do you want help?" station (a place to talk and help each other, equipped with baskets of mentor texts and cushions to sit on), for children to choose as they needed. Amanda's intention was to give long, uninterrupted time for children to become deeply involved in their learning. The time allowed children to use their agency: to be decision makers, problem solvers, collaborators, and creators. It allowed them the time to initiate and lead their own learning, rather than follow the teacher's directions all day long.

In the primary classrooms of my everyday research, child-initiated and child-led learning experiences were given more time than teacher-led experiences. For some, this took a workshop approach, with a short (five to ten minutes) teacher-led experience (often called the "mini-lesson") followed by much longer time (typically thirty to fifty minutes) for child-led exploration and creation. For example, Angela's reading workshop would usually begin with a teacher-led experience, such as a read-aloud or shared reading, in which she intentionally thought aloud and engaged children in thinking and talking about, for example, the characters' feelings, deepening inferential comprehension. For the next thirty minutes, the five- and six-year-old readers were given time to read self-selected texts alone and together. Some listened to audiobooks as they read along with the pages. Some lay on their bellies, huddled together, reading all about snakes and lizards. Others curled up on cushions in a private space to read a stack of favorite and familiar books. Angela conferred with children individually or in small groups. This one-on-one time told the children, "You are important enough and are doing such interesting learning that I want to spend some time *just with you* to learn more and support you." The reading workshop would conclude with a sharing circle, where children would talk about what they learned or enjoyed or thought about the texts they were reading. Angela's role was to listen, support participation, and gently nudge children's metacognitive thinking and sharing.

See video of Angela Kernahan's independent reading time, which shows the children collecting their book boxes (containing texts they have selected) and then choosing their reading spot for the day. You'll also see Angela conferring with some children during this time.

https://youtu.be
/dO7qcJ1KyXY

Similarly, Megan's mathematics lesson begins with a short teacher-led experience that often poses a problem or a wondering for children to solve, something that provokes children's thinking. It might also include some singing and a group experience that builds mathematical fluency. After ten minutes, the young mathematicians set off around the room with manipulatives of all sorts, some working alone and some with a friend.

One day as I was observing, Megan led a mathematics lesson with a group of seven- and eight-year-olds. The children gathered in a circle near the screen, and Megan began with a visual warm-up, a slide showing various numbers of fish in bowls. She asked, "What division story does this show?" and children turned and talked with each other. Some children collected whiteboards to help with their thinking. This was optional. Children knew by now that if the whiteboards and markers helped their thinking, they were always available. They used their agency to initiate their own learning process. After about ten minutes of problem solving and sharing, Megan introduced the mathematics challenge for the day, and children proceeded to learn alone or in pairs, with access to loose parts, hundreds charts, multiplication charts, and other manipulatives to support their thinking if they chose.

Your Everyday Research

▶ Write out the flow of how you spent the day with children. What do you notice? Do you have long, uninterrupted times for play and exploration, or does the day feel divided up into many smaller parts?

▶ How can you increase play and exploration times? Can you add five or ten minutes as a starting place?

▶ How long are you asking children to be in circle times or group meetings that are teacher directed? Does this time feel too long or just right to you? What is the children's behavior communicating to you? If you need to work hard to hold children's attention during this time, it is probably too long. How can you change this? (My general recommendation is for approximately ten minutes of teacher-directed time before children play, explore, and create. With some groups, this needs to begin with five minutes.)

The Physical Environment

My study of the educational project in Reggio Emilia, Italy, has deepened my understanding of the importance of the physical learning environment. Educators there famously call the environment the "third teacher" to acknowledge its value and importance. Curating the physical environment is seen as an aspect of pedagogy, not an added extra. With this in mind, I knew I needed to better understand the kinds of physical environments these cultures of agency inhabited. To research, I pulled up all the photographs from the preschools and primary school classes I had visited onto my computer screen and made a slideshow. I sat back and watched, resisting the urge to write notes at first.

As the images flowed past me, I saw how each physical environment was unique, but there was a definite thread running through them all. The best way I can describe this thread is to use the word *deinstitutionalized*. I first thought about this concept when reading Jim Greenman's work and continue to be challenged by this quotation (Greenman 2005, 64):

> Total institutions control space, time (e.g., hospital time), privacy, property, relationships, activities, and tend to treat people uniformly as subservient, in the name of health and safety.

Every time I read these words, I get an uncomfortable feeling in my gut. This is the opposite of what we want for children! Yet so many of our learning spaces (dare I say it, especially in primary schools) remain institutional, with rows or groups of desks, seating assigned by the teacher, and commercial charts covering the walls.

The agentive communities I visited were far from being institutional. The educators had spent a great deal of time and energy intentionally curating and creating a space that was warm, inviting, and interesting. They were unique and not a mere copy of ideas from Pinterest. Some were very home-like; all had some elements of homeyness. Like any home, the spaces spoke of the identity of the people who lived there: the children and educators. Perhaps that's a way of thinking of the physical space: a home for agency, connection, and learning.

See video of Ngutu College Year 1–3 Learning Spaces curated by Marcia, Liz, Angela, and Diane. You'll also notice how Megan has curated the learning space in the video of her "soft start" to the day.

https://youtu.be /JaLkTw54QbQ

Some ways educators intentionally deinstitutionalized the physical environment include these:

- Harsh overhead lighting was kept to a minimum, and lamps created a soft mood or highlighted an interesting display or play invitation.
- Colors were considered as you would for your home. Humans react to color, and color can affect our mood and emotional state, so this is an important consideration. Deinstitutionalized spaces feel calm, warm, and relaxed. Most of the spaces I spent time in featured muted, natural color palettes, the kind of colors you would be happy to decorate your home office or study with. Accents can be brighter, often leaping out from cushions and artworks by the children. The children bring the color to a space. Too much white can feel cold and institutional. Conversely, imagine how you would feel working in an office with four red walls and royal blue carpet. I think it would be hard to focus and concentrate. Yet

so many spaces created for children continue to be dominated by bright primary colors. In contrast, none of the learning spaces in my everyday research were dominated by primary colors. They might have had some bright accents, but the overall tone was warm and calm, created by the more natural palette.

- There was no clutter. This was true in *every* space I visited. As the saying goes, there was a place for everything and everything in its place. The educators understand that physical clutter also clutters energy for connecting, learning, and becoming deeply involved. Children had access to materials, but anything that was not being used was stored away, either in cupboards within the classroom or in another storage space. Just as in any home, there can never be too much storage!

- The educator's materials were also organized and did not take over the space. None of the primary classes had a traditional teacher's desk (these aren't often found in Australian preschools anyway). Megan used a shelf in the corner of the room for the materials she needed for teaching during the day. Angela used a cupboard and a basket under the stand for big books.

- The tone of each space was enhanced by soft furnishings and natural materials. Every class brought nature inside, whether it was a branch for hanging interesting creations, a jar of fresh herbs from the kitchen garden, or river stones with children's names on them for the morning roll call and feelings check-in.

- Preschools created spaces for exploration and play within larger rooms. There was a strong connection between indoors and outdoors (something very common and highly valued in Australian preschools). Invitations to play and explore were thoughtfully curated: materials were in good condition, extra materials were removed ("less is more" was a common mantra), and spaces were created for individual, small-group, and larger-group play.

- Primary classrooms were very similar to the preschool spaces. Some visitors to these primary or elementary spaces have been quite taken aback when entering, expecting desks in rows or groups, with a school-issued traditional desk and chair for each child and a large teacher desk at the front. They have commented that the classroom looks more like a preschool environment. Again, each room was unique, but each educator had intentionally created a layout where desks were not the first thing you noticed as you entered. Instead, at the door, you were greeted by the sight of play invitations, a welcome table with a vase of native flowers and the First Nations acknowledgment, a reading nook with shelves (book covers facing out) and cushions, shelves of puzzles and loose parts, and a dramatic play area of some sort. Among this richness, there were also tables of different heights where children could choose to work. (Individual student desks with metal legs and a tray underneath, like I've seen in many schools in the United States, are not a common feature in Australian schools, but school-issued desks with laminated tops in primary colors and standard heights are more common.)

- Whether preschool or primary school, the spaces included a large area for the group to sit together in a circular shape. In preschools, this was often several spaces for the small groups to gather for circle time with their primary care educator. This included smaller rugs in a book corner or block area, around a table outside, under a veranda, or on a picnic rug in the shade of a tree. The teachers frequently sat at the same level as the children. The space for a circular shape is significant for creating a culture of belonging and connection. If we are committed to children learning with and from each other and to creating the conditions for shared power, then this space is essential. The circle symbolizes democratic values of equality and respect. It is very difficult to engage in a dialogue with someone when you're facing the back of their head, as when you are sitting in rows facing the teacher at the front.

- Each space spoke to the unique identity of its members. Educators ensured that each child could see themselves and their culture in the space. Philomena and Kylie placed photographs of children (sometimes with their families) in frames around the room. Katie and the children displayed self-portraits with names in alphabetical order on the walls. This served a dual purpose as an alphabet chart as well as a proclamation of the identity of the space. What the spaces *didn't* include were commercially produced charts. The walls spoke the words and identity of the children. They reflected the conversations, thinking, and learning that had taken place within the space, declaring, "This is who we are and what we're interested in."

All-Access Pass

The final thing worth noting from my everyday research is how each teacher created the opportunity for children to access what they needed, when they needed it. This was a very strong thread through the diverse spaces. Mimi and her colleagues ensure children can access mark-making materials, glue guns, and tape by placing them on open shelving. Children find digging tools, planks, and buckets for the large sandpit in a crate nearby. Again, less is more. The main reserves of paint, paper, and extra markers are stored away in a cupboard. Extra outdoor loose parts are stored in a garden shed with a roller door that provides easy access for children accompanied by an educator. On the shelves are baskets and jars with just enough for children not to feel a sense of scarcity and also not feel overwhelmed with too much choice. This intentional curation of the environment means children are able to use their agency. When they have an idea, they can act on it *without* the teacher. They can initiate their own learning because they don't need to ask for materials.

Of course, sometimes a child will want to use something that is not available. Or the paint pots have run dry. Or an educator will intentionally extend or provoke learning by introducing a new material. At these times, the educators respond promptly to help the child access what they need. Most often this includes bringing the child with them to the storeroom so the child is involved in selecting the materials needed. Always the message is, "You are in control of your learning, and I'm here to help you."

The primary educators also ensured children had access to self-select materials, just like Mimi's team. However, it's also important to acknowledge that primary educators work in a different context from preschool educators. Most often primary classes include one teacher and twenty to thirty children. (Some Australian schools have begun to include a co-educator for each learning group or class. This is something I applaud!) The point is, the context is different, and it is not as easy for the one teacher to help every child when they need new materials or a new pencil. All the more reason to think carefully about how the environment provides for an "all-access pass" for materials when children need them.

From my years of teaching in primary schools, I know one of the most common irritations or friction points teachers face is when a child doesn't have a marker to use or their pencil is unsharpened. In a compliant culture, routines are dependent upon the adult, who must sharpen the pencil or find a new marker. Educators who build cultures of agency instead spend time at the beginning of the year establishing and practicing routines so children can independently get a new marker or sharpen a pencil. Children know where the extra stores are and understand they are trusted to get what they need when they need it. The carefully thought-out rituals for accessing materials prevent accidentally creating a culture of scarcity, where children are afraid that materials and supplies will run out. This not only allows for learner agency but also frees the teacher to confer with and support other children—that is, to teach.

In just the same way, children are trusted with their own hydration and toileting. In Australian preschools, children have open access to bathrooms all day, and there is no need for all children to be taken there together for a bathroom break. Children learn how to read their bodies and go to the toilet when their bodies signal they need to. The physical layout of the site enables this to happen safely.

Water is also always available, and children are encouraged to access it whenever they want. Many preschools have a self-serve snack ritual, where children can access a piece of fruit for snacktime when they want it. Again, this helps each child learn to read their body's signals for hunger.

Each primary teacher had their own way of ensuring children could get water and go to the bathroom whenever they needed to. Katie has a shelf for children's water bottles, and the children can access this whenever they need to during the day. They do not have to wait for a recess break to hydrate. I used to teach children the Auslan or American Sign Language sign for bathroom so they could quickly let me know they were going to the bathroom (they weren't asking for permission) without interrupting what I was exploring with another child. Angela has a set of break cards on lanyards that children can wear as they go to the bathroom, replacing the lanyards as they return. When trusted to take this responsibility, children rise to the occasion. And if the learning opportunities offered are interesting and engaging, they won't be trying to get out of class, as maybe you and I did when we were in school!

Finally, in agentive classrooms, the other "all-access pass" lets children choose where they sit, lie, learn, and play. In agentive preschools, there are no rotations of children going to play centers or limits on how many children are in different areas. If a problem arises when an area is crowded or there aren't enough materials, teachers guide a conversation about possible solutions, asking children for ideas. The suggestions are treated with respect, and together they come to a resolution—this might be as simple as some children and the teacher gathering extra materials or setting up a similar experience in another area.

In the primary classes I visited, children were not given assigned seating that they always needed to return to. They were trusted to choose their learning spaces. From this one decision, I believe, children begin to build a mindset for agentive learning—they know that they are in charge of their learning, and they can make decisions about it. They know that they can do more than wait to be told what to do and how to do it. I think it is significant that *not one* of the educators I observed, particularly in primary school settings, assigned seating to each child.

Allowing children to choose their learning place can be the first step in creating an environment that supports learner agency. Begin with the intention *not* to allocate seating and speak with the children about how you will trust them to make the best choice for their learning. Discuss what this will look, sound, and feel like. Support children to reflect on what will best help them focus. You might share what you know about your own learning, which conditions help you when you want to focus on a task at hand. Then observe what happens.

Over time children will build self-awareness and figure out what works best for them. The learning experience is important, more than the learning spot. You can ask, "Which place will help you to grow and learn the most?" Again, if there is a problem, see this as an opportunity for children to gain a better understanding of themselves as learners.

One conversation I overheard between Megan and a child illustrated this. India was finding it difficult to settle into her learning on this particular morning. Megan approached, crouched down beside India, and quietly said, "I can see that you're having trouble getting started today. Let's think about what you could do to help you get started without interrupting Amil's learning next to you. Would you like me to help you think of some options?"

India nodded. I don't think she had the words to express how she was feeling that morning.

Megan continued, "You could choose a different learning space, one where you feel you can focus. It might be somewhere on your own for a while. Or you could get a drink of water and see if that helps you focus when you come back to what you're doing. Or you could choose to have some time on our quiet time-out cushions until you're ready to get started."

These strategies were well known to the class, and India had used them before.

Megan paused, then asked, "What do you think? What will you choose?"

India chose to move to the quiet time-out cushions, with a cuddly toy and a small lava lamp to watch. After five minutes, she returned to the learning experience without any further support from Megan.

It's important to note that when Megan talks about her time-out cushions, *time-out* does not refer to a punishment, where a child is essentially placed in isolation. The spaces are for the child to have some time away, to use strategies to regulate any big emotions they are feeling, and to reset. They decide what helps them (a soft toy, watching the lava lamp, having a drink of water, or playing with a small focus toy, such as a squishy ball or popper fidget toy). And importantly, the child decides when they are ready to restart their learning experience with others. This practice is so powerful because it grants children emotional agency. Megan respects children and understands that all emotions are valid. Feelings aren't good or bad. She acknowledges children's big feelings and provides self-regulation strategies that will last them a lifetime.

Being intentional about the physical, temporal, and emotional environments we create is an essential part of creating a culture of agency. It's not an add-on. The deinstitutionalized space supports children's agency, well-being, and learning. It creates a secure and safe cocoon for being yourself, trying new things, and initiating learning.

CHAPTER 6

Contexts for Agency

People who feel a sense of agency in their lives think, "Yep. I can do that!" and then do it. They take action. They start things. In preschool and school, this means children have the self-efficacy, confidence, skills, and dispositions to initiate their learning. The opposite would have children paralyzed, not starting their explorations or creative processes because they're waiting for a set of instructions or directions from the adults.

My everyday research led me to wonder, "What kinds of learning contexts support this agency?" A learning context is often something physical that has been intentionally curated and set up by the educator, like the sandpit, dramatic play center, or block area. It can also be a particular experience that the educator intentionally plans for and gives time to, such as a read-aloud or circle game. It is where learning happens. I wondered:

- Is there a pattern or thread of similarity among the varied preschools and primary classrooms that value learner agency?
- What kinds of learning contexts or experiences did these "educators for agency" prioritize?
- What kinds of learning contexts or experiences did *not* feature in their days?
- What characteristics, qualities, or features typical to these contexts can I draw out from my observations?

To research, I returned to my notebook and my collection of videos and photos. I wrote some characteristics of each setting on individual sticky notes. I started with Mimi's preschool, then Megan's Year 3 class, then Danni's Year 1/2 class, and so on. I sorted the sticky notes into like categories and discovered that these characteristics were the most repeated:

- complex
- inclusive
- social
- active
- process-focused

Let's make sure we understand what each of these means as we peek into the learning contexts that embody these characteristics every day.

Complex

The learning contexts that empowered children to initiate and drive their learning were complex. They might have sometimes appeared simple, but they were not *simplistic* because of the learning that resulted and the great intentionality of the educators in planning, preparing, and proposing the learning experience.

Learning contexts need to provide something worthy of children's time, energy, and thought. They need to provide something worthwhile for children to do and therefore to use their agency toward. When the context has complexity, children think critically and creatively. This thinking is purposeful, sophisticated, and definitely in children's wheelhouses. After all, their natural way of learning—play—is filled with all kinds of critical and creative thinking!

The educators I observed did not shy away from exploring big ideas with children either. They knew young children were capable of thinking about the big ideas that affect their lives, like death, birth, bullying, friendship, climate change, racism, sexism, and justice. They live in this world, have a right to their opinions, and have a right to have those opinions be heard and respected. Their educators didn't hold them back or steer them to other topics because they were too young to discuss such things. As Peter Johnston and colleagues say in the marvelous book *Engaging Literate Minds*, "We should *not* expect children to be held in place by intellectual hierarchies" (Johnston et al. 2020, 1).

In an agentive culture, all topics are accessible to all learners (within developmentally appropriate guidelines). Being only four years old shouldn't mean you're not permitted to talk about a big topic like death. It affects everyone at some stage, after all. Four- and five-year-olds, when sparked by their curiosity, can expertly explore scientific concepts such as gravity, biodiversity, adaptation, and climate change. An agentive culture does not believe in hierarchies of knowledge that exclude some topics or participants just because of age or a preconceived idea that children "aren't ready for that yet." These social and intellectual hierarchies limit the conditions for agency. They create barriers to full participation. When the culture divides between "some who know" and "those who don't know," it restricts confidence, trust, and ultimately a child's motivation to use their agency in initiating learning and offering ideas.

Amber shares a powerful story from Ngutu College, a school that respects the child's right to have opinions and also supports them to take action and use their agency.

Jonnie's mum was going to a march organized in the city for International Women's Day. Jonnie, age six, was given the opportunity to go with her mum but decided that she would rather be at school. When they came to school, Jonnie and her mum spoke to me about an idea that Jonnie had. They could have the best of both worlds and organize a march at school! I responded that this was a great idea and helped Jonnie get the type of cardboard and paint she wanted. As she started making signs, a couple of other children joined in. They decided that the march would be at second break. I suggested that this would be an excellent announcement to include in our morning care circle so others knew it was happening. Not only did they announce it to our own class, but the group also decided they needed to tell all the classes!

At second break, a small group of four started marching around the yard and chanting. It wasn't long before more children joined, until there were children from Year 1 to Year 6 marching around the college, telling us that they wanted justice for women, now!

"It's about justice for women," Jonnie told us all.

"What does *justice* mean?" I asked.

"It means like . . . good," she replied.

A context that has little or no complexity does not support children in claiming their agency. There's little room for their thinking, decision-making, innovation, or reasoning. When children are provided with a template craft experience, they copy the model and follow the directions but cannot bring their creative thinking to it. When the context is too narrow, there is little room for children to generate ideas, evaluate their learning processes, reflect, and synthesize. Open-ended, complex contexts provide much more fodder for children's thinking and therefore bring deeper engagement.

When planning and preparing for learning contexts, the teachers gave considerable thought to providing for multiple possibilities. Rarely did the educator have a set, specific, product-focused outcome in mind. When there was a product, as when using the bookmaking approach to literacy, there was ample room for children's critical and creative thinking so that each product was as unique as the child who created it. The complexity came from the myriad ways children could explore and show their learning.

The materials carefully selected for children were also complex and open-ended. In contexts for agency, materials and play props allow for multiple possibilities. They can be transformed. For example, instead of dress-up clothes that dictate the roles children will play (as in a princess, superhero, or firefighter), agentive cultures value role-play materials that can be used in many different ways. Imagine a long piece of fabric such as a large scarf. Then think of as many things as possible the fabric can be transformed into during children's pretend play. You'd better stop at ten so you can continue reading! What was on your list? Here's a section of mine: hair, belt, sling, picnic rug, blanket for doll, wrap for doll, leash for dog, water, sash, holder for sticks, tablecloth, head covering, skirt, superhero cape . . .

The fabric allows children to use their agency as well as symbolic functioning to transform it into whatever their play needs. And tomorrow it can become something entirely different!

Your Everyday Research

Audit the materials you make available to children. Reflect on their open-endedness and complexity. Can they be transformed by children, or are they specific to one purpose? Use the following as provocative questions to nudge your thinking:

- ► Dress-up. Do you have materials and play props that dictate roles or ones that can be used for different roles and purposes? Think about how you can bring more open-ended materials into the area. What can be removed?
- ► Home or kitchen play. Do you have tubs of plastic food that can only represent one item? (A plastic sandwich is pretty well always going to be a sandwich.) Can you replace some of these with items that children can transform into different foods? Many educators I know use natural materials for play, so children use their symbolic functioning to transform a river stone, string, or twig into a banana, pasta, or a cup of tea.
- ► Construction. Can you supplement your wooden blocks with other loose parts? Imagine the possibilities when you add string, fabric, and recycled materials to the block area.

I recall observing Dannielle carefully prepare for mark-making in the studio space. The easels were placed side by side to encourage children to talk to each other as they made marks, also allowing for collaborative projects if they so desired. Several colors of paint were available on a small table between the easels. Each color had a paintbrush, and there was a small bucket of water for washing them. Dannielle and her colleagues had modeled for children how (if they chose) they could place two or more colors of paint on a baking tray to mix their own unique colors. Nearby there were multiple sizes of brushes and more paper for children to choose from. Here is a context with multiple possibilities. The opposite might be a context where children are given a template to paint or are directed to paint a particular "something"—a product defined by the adult—rather than being open to what the children do and how they think with materials.

Megan's mathematics lessons in Year 3 are just as open-ended. I shared a little about this in chapter 5, highlighting how children have open access to choose the materials they know will support their thinking. Megan designs the learning context with mathematical concepts in mind. She also considers how the context can offer complexity and open-endedness. Megan designs challenges that are open for multiple possibilities, and each day, her mathematics challenge invites children to engage in critical and creative thinking as mathematicians. One day as I observed, Megan offered the challenge, "How many different ways can we divide thirty-six?" Megan says, "The challenge is not about knowledge retrieval but either building understanding or applying mathematical concepts."

Some children applied the mathematics challenge to a real-life situation to make it meaningful for themselves. They drew pictures that were linked to their interests or to experiences in which they thought they'd use division, such as cooking. Others got out materials and used a trial-and-error approach to make equal groups. Some were interested in applying the division of thirty-six to a shape. Still others used their understanding of multiplication to figure out possibilities on whiteboards. Megan prompted children to explore their theories and the connection between multiplication and division, testing their theories to provide evidence.

Contexts that are complex allow for complex thinking. They allow for and expect children to use their agency within the experience. The opposite would be learning materials, questions, and invitations that are too obvious, such that you don't have to think much to know what to do, allowing little or no room for children's creativity, problem solving, or agency. Complexity requires intentional teaching, planning for there to be multiple possibilities and not just one way to achieve something.

Inclusive

An inclusive context welcomes, acknowledges, and respects diversity. In an early learning setting, this means learning experiences need to make a place for all kinds of learners. When contexts are open-ended, they are also more likely to be inclusive, because there are multiple ways for children to enter into the learning. There are multiple ways for them to exit the context too! By this I mean there are many ways for children to show their learning. Being inclusive helps multiage settings work as well.

Just like Megan's mathematics lesson, Angela's reading workshop is an inclusive context. All kinds of readers are welcomed and valued. Angela supports the learning of children ages six to eight, and they all find a place to be successful. Whether you are decoding words or reading illustrations (visual text), starting your first chapter book with the support of an audio-book, or voraciously reading a long series of books, you have a place here. Angela's intentional teaching focuses on strategies that can be applied across texts. She works in small groups and holds individual conferences where she can teach the "just right" strategy for each reader. She also connects young readers together by reading aloud picture books where they all can discuss big questions like "Why does the pigeon want to drive the bus, anyway?" or "Where do land mines (like the one Mali steps on in *One Step at a Time*) come from? Why are they there? Do we have any in Australia?"

Angela makes inclusion possible because she empowers choice. Children are taught how to choose books that are just right for them and then are trusted to make that choice. Being "just right" isn't about a certain level though. It's about whether the text is interesting to the reader, whether they want to talk about it after reading, and whether the reader can construct meaning from the multimodal nature of pictures and words working together.

Similarly, the educators I observed favored a bookmaking approach to literacy. Bookmaking is inclusive because everyone can find a way to feel and be successful. By their nature, picture books are multimodal. The illustrations and words work together to communicate meaning. Thus, all forms of mark-making are valued as communication, and this learning context affirms that the three-year-old making marks on a page is communicating. The marks may represent a person (like dad), an object (a house or a monster), a movement (zoom-zoom of a car), or a feeling (bold, heavy lines for anger). I have seen children use all these forms of representation in their bookmaking. As children grow and learn more about the alphabetic system, their mark-making begins to show shapes that are proudly proclaimed to be writing. We often call this "zigzag writing" or "loop-de-loop writing." Very soon, letter-like shapes appear, then random strings of letters. It's so exciting to observe children's developing knowledge of the alphabetic principle (graphemes and phonemes) emerge on the pages of their books. The young bookmakers use their agency to create and communicate with drawings and words, both spoken and written. Everyone has a place in bookmaking. Everyone is growing as a writer, starting from where they are right now.

See video of bookmaking workshop with Angela's Year 1-3 group, where you'll see young authors working on a variety of books about topics they have chosen.

https://youtu.be /aiTldebLlw0

Within agentive contexts, approximations are valued and encouraged not only in literacy but also in science, technology, engineering, and mathematics (STEM); the arts; sports; and all areas of learning and development. Cast your mind back to when you learned something new. Perhaps you recall learning to drive (remember those first attempts at turning a corner or parking?) or perhaps you recall taking a dance class or learning a musical instrument. We park too far from the curb. Our first dance steps are very wobbly, and our initial attempts at a new song are slow or disjointed. We all approximate as we learn new things. This is why I prefer the term "approximated spelling" to "invented spelling"—children are using what they know at that time to approximate. With practice and experience, these approximations grow closer to the conventional. I'm sure you can now park a car near the curb with relative ease! In agentive cultures, approximation is valued as a strong learning strategy, not seen as getting something wrong.

Social

Agentive contexts also allow for and appreciate social learning. That doesn't mean that children always learn with others. There are plenty of times when children choose to learn alone, and at times they are encouraged to do so by their teachers. But these solo pursuits are intertwined by a strong thread of belonging to a community of learners. The teachers prioritize opportunities to share thinking, ideas, and artifacts of learning. They understand that this time is critical to learning with and from each other. They want children to understand that adults are not the only teachers, to instill the belief in children that they can learn from each other, not just from the grown-ups in the room.

In the spaces I visited, these repeated routines of sharing thoughts became rituals because of the huge amounts of intentional teaching they contained. I witnessed Turn and Talk (or Triads) techniques, when children conversed with partners for a few minutes and then shared their ideas with the wider group. Another sharing ritual I saw was a No Hands Up protocol, as detailed in chapter 4. It was very common for the group of children and their educator to sit in a circle to facilitate listening to each other's ideas. Reflection circles and share times featured at the end of many writing, reading, or mathematics lessons. Mimi's preschool team finished the day with small groups of children sitting on the floor (indoors or out), reflecting on the day together. In Mimi's setting, there was always plenty of time set aside for sharing the books created by three- and four-year-old authors.

Within these sharing rituals, educators support children to learn the metalanguage of being an agentive learner or, in other words, to have the language to describe and share their learning. Educators intentionally model their own thinking, using language that the children quickly adopt as their own, for example, "I'm wondering . . ." and "Hmm . . . that's so interesting. Could you please tell us more?"

Sharing rituals also build metacognitive awareness and increase the likelihood that learning will stick and be transferable. As Vygotsky (1978, 88) famously said, "Children grow into the intellectual life around them." The children I observed were immersed in a rich intellectual life where all group members (children and adults) share ideas, wonder, question, and feel amazed, curious, and surprised about all kinds of things. The overall feeling was, "We grow our thinking together."

Active

Contexts for agency are active in many ways, including physically. Children build with blocks and construct with loose parts. They use mathematics manipulatives to deepen conceptual learning. They create texts in their play and mark-making. They make books. They walk, jump, roll, skip, and climb as they stretch themselves physically.

A very strong pattern emerged in my research as I was sorting through my notes, photos, and videos. In the spaces with a culture of agency, children moved throughout the day. This might be expected when we are talking about young children. Have you ever had to ask a three-year-old to stay still in a seat while you're at an appointment? But not too long ago—and dare I say, perhaps still in some schools—children as young as four or five were expected to stay in one seat for long periods of time. I understand the real pressure educators feel to push down academic learning, but in our consultancy work, we strive to push up early childhood values and pedagogical principles. Sitting still for long amounts of time is the antithesis of agentive learning. It is impossible to use your agency, develop self-efficacy, and initiate learning when you're asked to stay in one place, like at a desk, for a certain amount of time.

As I mentioned earlier, *not one* of the primary teachers I observed allocated seating for children in the class. Children could choose where they learned: standing at a high table or sitting on the floor, on large cushions around a coffee table, or at a more conventional table. Children were trusted to choose the best place for themselves to learn. Alongside that, they were rarely asked to stay in that place. If they chose to move to another spot, that was fine. Of course, these are regular five- to eight-year-olds: some children benefited from extra support to make the strongest choice for their learning. Within a short amount of time, though, most children were making responsible decisions for where they learned and how they moved from space to space as they needed. They learned how to make these decisions because they were trusted to do so. They were not expected to learn this immediately on day one, and educators interpreted their approximations as steps in the growing process.

High-quality Australian preschools are filled with movement! The only time I witnessed children being encouraged not to move (too much) was during a rest time in one child care setting. Each child had their own low cot (which they could climb on and off themselves). They were gently encouraged and supported to stay on their cot during rest time. But they weren't forced to nor disciplined if they did not sleep. Children could choose to read a book, cuddle a teddy, or listen to quiet music. The focus was on community responsibility. We want to be quiet so the other children who need to sleep can do so. We want to do this because we belong together and care about each other.

Movement also benefits children's development of executive functioning. This is a set of skills that helps us focus, plan, prioritize, work toward goals, self-regulate, and evaluate. Executive functions act like our own orchestral conductor, coordinating different parts to work together in harmony. Our internal conductor needs to coordinate a number of cognitive, behavioral, and emotional tasks. It includes functions for inhibitory control (the ability to control impulses), working memory (the ability to store and manipulate information in one's short-term memory to use while engaged in a task), cognitive flexibility, time management, planning, and organization. We can also think of executive functioning as "learning to learn" skills, our learning muscles.

John R. Best from the Department of Psychology at the University of Georgia cites numerous studies that demonstrate the connection between physical activity and executive functioning, concluding, "Recent experimental research indicates that both acute and chronic aerobic exercise promote children's executive function" (Best 2010, 331). *Acute* exercise refers to the effects observed after one exercise experience, and *chronic* refers to the ongoing, cumulative effects of regular aerobic exercise. Exercise helps get blood and oxygen flowing to the brain, supporting emotional well-being and the development of "learning to learn" skills. Physical games, finger-plays, dances, and circle games also help children develop working memory, inhibitory control, and organization (Calderon 2020).

When playing the circle game "Alice the Camel," children join in the song and clap together, developing their ability to wait for their turns to join the line of "camel humps" in the circle. As they sing and move together in a familiar context, they hold the words, rhythm, and rules of the game in their minds. A myriad executive functioning skills are used and developed. It's no wonder that singing and movement featured in all the early learning settings I observed.

See videos of outdoor learning contexts of St. Margaret's Kindergarten, Woodville, South Australia, where you'll see children initiating their own learning experiences, gathering materials for their endeavors in inclusive, social contexts full of opportunities for movement.

https://youtu.be /pkPC6GpY1cw

Process-Focused

Contexts for agency focus on the learning that takes place during the *process* of creating, making, doing, thinking, and communicating. They do not place sole focus on the end product. That's not to say the end product is of no importance. When you are creating a spaceship from large loose parts, having a vision for the end product is important, particularly for those involved in the creative act. However, educators who care about learner agency understand that if they focus too much on what the product of learning looks like, they will prevent children from doing the thinking and creating themselves. There will be too much of the adults' and too little of the children's ideas in what comes about. Children will be robbed of the chance to see themselves as capable creators, mathematicians, poets, or sculptors. Their identity as capable and agentive learners is not nurtured when they are creating something that needs to fit in with their teachers' ideas.

One of the biggest misconceptions about taking a pedagogical stance that values play and inquiry is that it results in a free-for-all. Nothing could be further from the truth! Contexts for agency are also contexts for play and inquiry. They are not so open-ended and laissez-faire that anything goes. That would leave very little for educators to do but set out and pack up materials! Let's take a look at the vital and sophisticated role of educators when they care about the learning process more than the look of the final product.

Educators prepare contexts for agency with great intention. They think about their hopes for the learning and development of the children they work with. They consider the best open-ended materials to support this learning. But it doesn't end there. They also consider how to present or propose the learning context to children. Some contexts are presented as they are, such as the painting easels or the reading nook. Others are presented as an invitation or proposal for involvement. Often I observed teachers proposing a learning experience in the form of a big question.

Overwhelmingly, the words I most consistently heard from teachers were, "I wonder . . ." They took a curious stance in everything. They posed genuine open questions and shared their ponderings. They drew children into thinking about concepts and big ideas through active experiences and then theorizing about them together. The educators kept opening doors to learning one at a time and welcomed children through each door by thinking aloud and sharing their wonderings. The questions beckoned children forward. Of course, many of these questions came from the children; they weren't always from the teacher's mind. In this, the teacher's role is to illuminate a child's wondering so everyone can think about it together.

Penny shares a story of companionable learning, investigating alongside four-year-old Max, who sparked the learning with a wondering.

It was early in my days at the center, and it was also Max's first day. He was sticking fairly close to me, and we were outside wandering around together. Max climbed on the big "cotton reel" (a giant wooden spool that was previously used to store rope or wire) that I was leaning against, peered into the dark hole in the center, and asked, "What's in there?"

I had no idea, but he'd sparked my curiosity as I had never wondered about it.

"I don't know Max. How can we find out?"

That began a day of exploring what was in the hole, working out ways to discover and get the contents out of the hole. Our investigating naturally drew in other children along the way, and Max made friends as we explored.

I watched children develop and articulate theories about how things got in there and how we could get them out. I listened to their self-talk as they persevered and concentrated to find the right way to grip the long tongs to haul the treasure up through the cotton reel hole and into the light. I watched four-year-old Julian racing back across the mound with a second set of tongs he intended to use to retrieve a set he had unintentionally dropped to the bottom of the hole. He yelled, "I get it now!" as he pulled the tongs to the surface. When children give you the curriculum like this in the everyday, you need to be available to join in.

Penny was focused on the process of learning and, in doing so, was able to harness the energy for learning that Max's question sparked. It wasn't preplanned, but it certainly was intentional. Penny's intentions supported Max to engage in a process of inquiry: to investigate, wonder, form theories, and then test and trial them. She was also intentional in supporting other children to join the endeavor so that Max, on his first day at preschool, could begin to form relationships with other children. Penny's intentionality and her understanding of learning enabled her to follow Max and the other children, to support their undertakings, to nudge, and to wonder aloud *with* them in a genuine and authentic context. She supported their agency by being their learning companion.

If Penny were a teacher who did not understand the value and importance of children feeling a sense of agency in their learning, she might have shut down Max's initial question by telling him what was in the hole. Or she might have dismissed his wondering with "Nothing much is down there" or even "It's really dirty, so don't put your hands down there!" She might have ignored the question, thinking only of the planned activities for later and how they needed to go inside for a fruit break soon.

Each of the teachers I observed was attuned to the moments of wonder that children gifted them. They didn't always have time to follow the line of inquiry right in that moment, but they listened with respect and interest, often suggesting it could be explored later. Some primary educators asked children to write their wonderings on a whiteboard or chart on the wall so that they wouldn't be lost, and they would remember to explore them when there was more time.

Some particular contexts provide for every agentive characteristic by being complex, inclusive, social, active, and process-focused. These contexts provided another thread of continuity throughout the preschools and schools in my research group, as particular learning contexts were valued by each of the educators and featured highly in their intentional teaching. I've woven stories about these contexts throughout the book, but I think it's worth naming them clearly. This does not mean I think these are the only contexts for agency, but these were prominent in my research:

- pretend play
- inquiry- and project-based learning
- loose parts play
- bookmaking
- reading and talking about books every day in the form of independent reading, book clubs, or interactive read-alouds
- mark-making in various modes
- open-ended mathematics investigations

See video of story play with Marcia's Year 1–3 group.
You'll notice all the characteristics of an agentive learning
context here.

https://youtu.be
/az_WxpqyenM

Your Everyday Research

► What *wouldn't* you consider an agentive context for learning? Which types of learning tasks could be classed as a *compliant* context?

► Consider each of the learning contexts above. Are you already including these in your intentional teaching?

► Are you interested in learning more about one of the learning contexts mentioned?

► Reflect on the learning contexts you create and offer children. How are they
  ▷ complex?
  ▷ inclusive?
  ▷ social?
  ▷ active?
  ▷ process-focused?

► Are there modifications you can make to bring more of these characteristics into the learning contexts and experiences you offer children?

CHAPTER 7

Educator Agency

By now you've met a number of inspiring educators on the pages of this book. Each has many qualities any employer would look for when choosing a staff member. They're hardworking, passionate, committed, reflective, and open to learning. And one more thing: they act with a sense of agency. Just like the children they work with, they are empowered to have a say in their work and to guide the direction of their days spent alongside children. The teachers have been supported to create rich communities where children thrive, largely because they have been encouraged and trusted to have agency as professionals.

Educator agency can be thought of as having the capacity and opportunity to actively shape our work with children and also our professional learning. Educators with a sense of agency initiate their work. That is, they innovate by trying out new ideas, observing, noticing, and reflecting on their theories. They have a self-awareness about their role as educators. That is, they engage in everyday research.

Agentive educators do not wait to be given a direction by their leader or to be told what program to use. They do not blindly accept any new initiative or commercial program that is presented to them. At times they will take a stand and advocate strongly for what they believe is best for children's learning and well-being.

Qualities of the Agentive Educator

Perhaps you're already reflecting on the times you've acted with a sense of agency. One of those times might have even been deciding to read this book! Think of the times when you have made a professional judgment, such as implementing a new direction with a child or bringing a new pedagogical practice to your teaching. Think of the times that you've reflected on ways to grow your teaching, perhaps striving to ask stronger questions or changing the way you facilitate the morning meeting because you wondered how much of it was "because we've always done it this way." These are times that you are acting with agency. The decisions were driven by something inside of you, not by an external force asking (or making) you do something. You had an itch, or a wondering, that sparked curiosity and drove your intrinsic motivation and agency to act.

The qualities of educators who act with agency include these:

- They have clear beliefs about learning and teaching (pedagogy). These beliefs are not so rigid that they are closed to changing and growing. The life of an educator is about continual evolution. I know my own beliefs have grown, changed, and become clearer as I have reflected, edited, and added to them over the years. Having clarity about your philosophy of learning and teaching gives you a compass for navigating the myriad messages thrown at education by the media, publishers, researchers, and bureaucratic systems.

- They carry a deeply held belief that all children can learn, viewing children through a strengths-based lens. This strengths-based view melds with your own philosophy to guide your decisions. When you're presented with a new idea, initiative, practice, or program, first reflect on the image of the child it embodies. Does it see children as capable and competent to have agency in their learning? Does it allow for child and teacher agency? Or does it "dumb down" learning so it becomes a technical completing-the-task set of activities? Are children capable of more than this practice or approach allows? How much of the thinking does it do for children, when they are capable of doing it for themselves?

- They are self-aware and reflective. The practice of reflection is like the practice of yoga: the more you practice it, the more it becomes habit and the more benefits you reap. I also think of self-reflection as *practice* in the verb sense because it is the repetition of an act: the act of returning to a past experience in your mind, evaluating it, and using it to form personal theories. Reflection enables you to make connections between your philosophy and your teaching practices. These are interdependent: your philosophy informs your teaching *and* your reflection on your teaching informs your philosophy. Educators who act with agency are aware of their strengths as teachers. They are also aware of possible areas for growth because they constantly reflect on their personal pedagogy.

- They have a commitment to continual professional development. Agentive educators crave continual growth in their teaching practices. They see teaching as both a craft and an art: creative; fluid; developing with time, practice, and reflection; and something that you bring so much of yourself to. They continue to evolve as educators for life. Teaching is more than a job for them; it is a vocation, a calling.

See videos of interviews with educators Katie Ashmead, Megan Fyffe, Amber Hall, Mimi Hayward, and Angela Kernahan. Here they talk about what learner agency means to them, how they plan for it, and why having agency as educators is so important to them.

https://youtube.com /playlist?list=PL7WB JrjC0IsIxhOSCtl _MhqReN5ykJeqA

Conditions for Educator Agency

Educator agency is not a given and cannot be taken for granted. Unfortunately, for many educators around the globe, opportunities for having a say in the ways they teach have diminished in recent years. In his book *Changing Australian Education: How Policy Is Taking Us Backwards and What Can Be Done about It*, Alan Reid (2019) attributes this trend to factors including the marketization of education, a greater emphasis on competition, increasing privatization, and a focus on measurable outcomes through standardized test scores.

Whether at a system level or a preschool or school level, when leadership is narrowly focused on standardized test scores, it results in standardized pedagogy. The pressure to improve test scores filters down from politicians and education ministers to directors and principals, and then down to teachers. This pressure makes leaders and teachers feel as if they need to implement strategies that promise quick results, which can often lead them to purchase a commercial program. I call this rise of commercial program use the "programatization of education," and I have witnessed it since I began my teaching career in 1985. I do understand why some turn to the commercial programs; they are seductively marketed and promise those elusive results. For some leaders, adopting a commercial program will ease real and constant pressure from their supervisors. But this trend is so dangerous. Commercial programs that dictate the lesson sequence, and even provide a script for teachers, support the antithesis of teacher agency. Commercial programs do not always allow teachers to use their professional knowledge or make pedagogical decisions for their group of diverse and beautifully complex learners. You can't have a sense of agency in your life or profession if you are told what to do and when and how to do it. Scripted programs leave no room for teachers' professional judgment or creativity. They leave no room for them to respond to children's thinking, to use their observations and formative assessments, or to *engage* in the reciprocal act of teaching and learning. I find the idea of "teacher-proofing" a curriculum to be highly offensive.

The stories I've shared with you come from preschools and schools that do not adopt commercial programs. They place the curriculum design firmly with the educators who know the children best. Their professional libraries contain resources for teachers to draw on, but program leaders do not expect educators to follow them robotically with no adaptation for group, culture, and site context. So, what are the conditions that these very different sites create for their teachers so they feel a sense of agency?

View of the Educator

In chapter 1, we briefly looked at the image of the child that teachers unconsciously hold and how it influences our words, our actions, and all those fifteen hundred decisions we make each day. Our image or view of the educator is just as important.

Returning to what I wrote about children in chapter 1, let's adapt the ideas to help us reflect on how we see our role as teachers. These reflective questions can be applied to our views of ourselves as well as to how the school, bureaucratic system, and society views educators.

- Are educators seen as empty and so need to be provided with scripted lessons to follow?
- Are educators seen as a threat to the power and control of a system or school, or to a leader's personal power? Do systems place restrictions and boundaries on what educators do because they can't be trusted?
- Are educators viewed as professionals, with the knowledge, experience, and wisdom to make decisions, design a curriculum, and create change?

If you are leading a team or community, I hope these questions help you to pause and reflect on what you believe, deep down, about the educators you work with each day. Our reflections must move beyond mere words, though. The actions, decisions, and structures—and yes, words too—that leaders use will either be loyal to or betray their views of educators.

Leadership

I am privileged to have long-term relationships with three of the communities whose stories fill the pages of this book: Ngutu College, Prospect North Primary School, and St. Paul Lutheran School. Their leaders view educators as professionals. They value the knowledge and experience educators bring with them, trusting educators to design a curriculum, curate learning contexts, and drive their professional learning.

This doesn't mean there are no guidelines and anything goes. Each school's philosophy, values, and image of the child guides decision-making. Teachers are expected to talk about the connections between their teaching practices and the vision of the school. There are threads of continuity but no cookie-cutter lessons across groups or classes.

Each school has organizational structures that provide opportunities for educators to reflect and talk with each other about learning and teaching:

- Collaborative teaching. Each primary or elementary class at Ngutu College is led by an educator and a co-educator (teaching assistant). Every day educators and co-educators reflect and plan together in their joint role of educating the children in that group. The multiple educators and co-educators on the integrated preschool-Foundation team in Madlurta at Ngutu also collaborate daily. At Prospect North, flexible spaces allow two or three classes (and therefore two or three educators) to work together each day. The flexible spaces at St. Paul Lutheran also offer opportunities for team-teaching, and leaders actively encourage this as an ongoing practice.

- Professional learning communities (PLCs). In PLCs, small groups of educators are formed so educators can direct their own professional learning, such as by collaborating and engaging in critical reflection together. PLCs seek to break down the isolation of teachers, particularly in primary and elementary schools. However, too often these are *learning* teams in name only. I've heard teachers complain that they don't have time for professional dialogue because the agenda of their PLC is hijacked by administrative tasks sent by the leadership team. When leading for teacher agency, opportunities must be given for educators to be in dialogue with each other. To be a true professional learning *team,* the agenda must be set by the participants. There may be parameters, such as a focus on a concept or an area of learning that connects everyone in the school, but the specifics must be worked out by the members of the group. This is where agency takes flight. Without directing the agenda, having a say in the specifics, or having time to explore, there is no room for teacher agency. The schools I observed that do not have PLCs instead bring the principles of agency, choice, and voice to staff meetings and other professional learning opportunities.

- Curriculum design. When leaders place the responsibility for curriculum design in the minds and hands of educators, agency thrives because teachers are trusted. Their professional knowledge and judgment are respected. Again, these agentive cultures are not so laissez-faire that anything is accepted: the pedagogy needs to connect to the school's philosophy and values. And teachers are not left to sink or swim in designing the learning path for children. Early-career teachers are mentored and supported in curriculum design. Staff members or consultants at each school lead professional learning. The three schools share a focus on collaborative planning and design: teachers do not work in isolation, and time is provided for this process.

As well as adopting specific organizational structures, agentive schools also build a culture that supports and promotes agency for all staff. Leadership takes particular responsibility for this, just like the preschool teacher or Year 2 teacher would do in creating the culture for their group or class. Like the teacher, agentive leaders are intentional in developing relationships of trust and prioritize time for this throughout the year.

When we understand agency as initiating learning and contributing ideas, a culture of identity and belonging is essential. In previous chapters, we explored how important it is for children to feel safe so they can contribute. We adults really are not that much different from children. Our sense of identity as educators grows through our relationships with each other. Creating a culture of agency for educators requires opportunities to be in open conversation. Just as we know it is important for children to have time to play, talk, and form connections with each other, educators benefit from times when they can be with each other and share their thinking without judgment. This might even start in social situations, such as a shared meal or a movie night together. It is only through repeated interactions that professional relationships can grow. It's difficult for the Year 2 teacher to feel a connection to the preschool teacher if they've never had much chance to talk.

In Australia schools have a room or lounge where staff (teaching and non-teaching) can retreat for a few minutes over recess or lunchtime. These places are important contexts for connection and belonging. Katie started at a new school right as COVID-19 restrictions meant that teachers were asked not to meet in the staff room for their own health and safety. As a result, there were colleagues on Katie's new staff with whom she did not have more than a passing conversation for months. The COVID-19 situation was extreme at the time, so it was the only right decision to be made in the best interests of staff. But Katie's experience made me think about how important the space and the opportunity for informal socializing is in forming a sense of belonging. Just as we want to provide children with uninterrupted time for play, knowing it will build secure relationships, educators need time and space for that too.

To use your agency—to take action, initiate, and contribute—you need to feel emotionally safe. As teachers, we feel this when we can trust that our ideas and contributions are respected. Sharing our ideas with others can make us feel vulnerable, but when we trust our colleagues and our leaders, the risk is minimalized. I don't see this as very different from the relationship of mutual trust between an educator and child, but I do wonder whether leaders give a lot of thought to it.

If you are leading a team or community, some strategies for developing trust and emotional security include these:

- Model being genuinely curious about teachers' ideas and thinking. Ask open-ended questions like, "I'm curious. What did you think about [the webinar last week]?" or "Tell me more about how you [decide to set up for loose parts play]."
- Listen with intention and without commenting when teachers are sharing their ideas. Sometimes people in leadership positions feel the need to share their thinking all the time. Some believe they are leading by doing a lot of talking. Some feel the pressure to prove to their teams that they have knowledge about the topic at hand. But the strongest leaders elevate others' voices, not only their own.
- Intentionally model your own learning, hypothesizing, and confusions. Be brave to share a time when you got it wrong, knowing that you are demonstrating how to be reflective. You are also setting the tone that it's okay to try something that doesn't work perfectly. The more we share our own "wonderful uneasiness," the safer it is for all team members to do so.

- Involve educators in decision-making. When exploring a new pedagogical approach or direction, frame it as a research project and involve educators in trialing it for a number of weeks. Ask them to record what worked and what didn't work, as well as the wonderings and questions that emerged. Then meet to share the everyday research and discuss the decision. Address such questions as: Does the new approach fit with our philosophy and values? Does it treat children as capable and allow for their agency? Do we want to adopt and use it? When educators are asked for their professional opinions about a new initiative, they are more likely to buy in, and more important, they will feel respected. A word of caution though: If teachers are consulted but the decision always goes with the status quo or what the leader wants, trust will erode. The consultation will feel hollow. So, consult only when there is a true and genuine option. If you've already made a decision (perhaps for good reasons), then don't pretend to consult. This will show educators only that you can't really be trusted to listen to their perspectives and professional opinions.
- Begin staff meetings with a ritual of belonging. We explored how important these are to children in chapter 3, but have you thought about creating them for your staff team too? Some examples are these:
  - ▸ Acknowledge the First Nations peoples of the land you are meeting on.
  - ▸ Share an inspirational quotation and provide five minutes to talk about it in small groups.
  - ▸ Sing a song together.
  - ▸ Take turns each meeting to choose and read a children's picture book.
  - ▸ Take turns each meeting to tell a story of a child's learning.
  - ▸ Take turns each meeting to choose and read a short poem.
  - ▸ Do a group word game or mathematics puzzle together.

Navigating Challenges

What if you're a teacher who craves more agency in your work? I hear you. It is incredibly challenging if you are part of a preschool or school that does not value or recognize educator agency. Perhaps you've been mandated to use a commercial program, or perhaps you feel that you can't try a new pedagogical practice because you fear your leadership will think it's not working. Perhaps you don't yet trust your leadership to see beyond the immediate if things don't go smoothly at first, or perhaps you're unsure whether your leadership understands or values the intentions you are bringing to your everyday research. I won't lie—these are difficult things to navigate.

But what *can* you do? The optimist in me wants to believe that no situation is hopeless and that there is a way to bring some agency into your work. After all, having a sense of agency is where we find meaning in what we do every day. Perhaps that's where to start.

What drives and motivates you to be an educator? What moments of learning and teaching do you love? These things give you life and energy and turn on your internal power to shine as an educator. It might be something like the joy of sharing a silly song with children or watching the creative thinking that happens when children explore loose parts. For me, it would be all of those and also reading picture books and playing circle games together. It is the joy of the aha look on a child's face when they figure out something on their own and feel a sense of achievement.

Once you're clear about what aspects of being a teacher bring you joy, look at each day or each week. Where can you carve out time for these life-giving moments? It might be once a day or once a week. If you're in a particularly rigid environment, it will probably be easier to carve out small moments of joy through singing or sharing a joke with children. It might be making a change to the scripted morning meeting to include a circle game. It might be planning a weekly loose parts play session. But don't underestimate how important this is. If it brings you joy, chances are it will bring joy to the children too.

Then be an advocate. You don't have to be loud and aggressive or the thorn in your leader's side to advocate for children's agency—and your own. My motto is always to start small and build on success. Choose one pedagogical practice you want to introduce (or reintroduce) into your teaching.

Once you've decided what you want to try, research it. The most powerful advocates have knowledge. Research the neuroscience of singing and its connections to reading. Or connect loose parts play to the STEM standards for your district. Once you are armed with some research, then you're ready to have a conversation with your leaders. Ask for a few minutes of their time because you're really excited about some research you've been reading or some thinking you've been doing about the connections between the standards and mandated curriculum. Explain what you've been thinking and hypothesizing about. You might find words like these helpful: "I read this, and it made me think . . ." or "I've been wondering how this will help children to . . ." Finally, ask if your leader would be a critical friend during your research project and if they can meet again in a few weeks' time when you'll share what you've been trying and what you've noticed about children's learning.

If you took charge and harnessed your agency in the most professional of ways, I wonder what would happen.

The Final Word from the Children

What do children think about being part of these thriving learning communities? It seems apt that we give children the final word. After all, this book is all about honoring and respecting their right to have a say in their learning and schooling experience. We asked children, "What is it like to belong to your class, and why?"

> "Belonging in our class means we do nice things together like our learning and investigations. We tell funny jokes to each other." —*Lily, 7*

> "We feel good in our class family because we all look after each other." —*Simrat, 6*

> "We are happy in our class family because we are all nice to each other and we treat our things with respect." —*Jolie, 7*

"We make each other laugh and we celebrate all of our differences." —*Anashay, 6*

"I love when new students come to our class so I can make more new friends." —*Indi, 6*

"We belong to our class family because we all work in a team together. We care for each other." —*Scarlett, 6*

"I like it because people respect our classroom by cleaning up." —*Harlow, 6*

"We treat other people how we want to be treated." —*Cayden, 6*

"The teachers help us and there's lots of things to do." —*Elijah, 4*

"Because I'm happy here playing with my friends." —*Milana, 5*

"I'm new, but I like it here because lots of people can help fill my bucket and I can fill other people's buckets too." —*Kaliti, 6*

"It's amazing because you [teachers] challenge us. I like that you are making our brains more smarter. I like that the whole group is just open and friendly." —*Shamshir, 6*

"I like it because there's so many books—it feels good." —*Dinuk, 6*

"We look after our toys and not break anything." —*Maddy, 4*

"I like this classroom because it looks really nice. It feels happy." —*Blair, 6*

"I like about Madlurta [preschool name] that we have lots of play spaces . . . treehouse . . . circus tent . . . Lego . . . reading spaces. We write our own books. The rocks there can hurt you. I like learning about Kaurna best." —*Mabel, 4*

"I like the marbles, the chess, and the games and they make me feel good. I feel helped and stable because people help you in this class." —*Alexander, 6*

"I like that Ms. Fyffe helps us to grow our brains and we get to watch beautiful videos. I like what we do, like writing and drawing and listening to Ms. Fyffe read." —*Olivia, 6*

"I like songs, games, bookmaking when I color and draw and write. I hate someone not playing with me. I like group time, going on the swings, the library, second break, books, reading." —*Layla, 4*

"It feels a bit nice. I like it because there are fun things to do. We always are friends." —*Nazhleen, 6*

It all comes back to relationships, doesn't it? The sense of belonging and being seen for who you are. I don't think there is a greater gift we can give to others than to say, "I see you, I know you, and you are enough just the way you are."

As six-year-old Nazhleen says, "We are an 'us' community."

Reflection and Goal-Setting Tool

I'm hoping the "Your Everyday Research" sections that are sewn within each chapter have supported you to reflect on your own context and your own pedagogical choices. I thought it would also be helpful to have a final reflection guide that you can easily pull out now or anytime in the future when you feel the need to revisit the ideas in this book. We're always growing and evolving as educators, so I sincerely hope this will be a tool for you in the future too.

There are many ways you can use this tool. It is designed to be as inclusive and open as the learning contexts we read about on these pages. You could take it as a whole, or, preferably, work through one section at a time so you don't feel pressure to rush through it. You can use it for personal reflection about your intentional teaching practices or use it as a team to reflect and evaluate your early childhood education and care service, preschool, or primary classroom.

My hope is that the questions serve as a guide for your thinking, not as a rating scale. In reflecting honestly about your current teaching practices, you'll unearth possible little irritations or wonderings. Use these to push yourself further. Embrace the "wonderful uneasiness," knowing this is you growing and evolving as an educator. It might immediately cause you to adopt a strategy you read about on these pages. Or it might nudge you to research other thinking about agency or executive functioning or the philosophy of Reggio Emilia. Make it work for you.

www.redleafpress
.org/aca/appendix
.pdf

Clarify Your Learning Culture

How clear are you about the kind of learning culture you want to create? Can you articulate this to others? Your intentional teaching starts here, in gaining clarity about what you hope to build with children and families.

Visualize the best day in your setting. You may not have had it yet! Imagine what it would be like if educators, children, and families were learning and collaborating at their optimal level. What does it look like when children are thriving in your setting? Write words and phrases from your mental image to help you articulate this.

I see children . . .	I see educators . . .

I see families . . .	I hear these words . . .

What kinds of learners do you hope to support? What dispositions and qualities do you hope to instill, support, and nurture?

What could this look like?

Disposition or Quality	What It Could Look Like
Example: resilient	• Children are comfortable with mistakes or approximations. • They pick themselves up from disappointments and have strategies for joining in again in different situations. • Children are comfortable with some struggle in their learning. They don't give up when they need to put in extra effort or at first don't succeed.

Relationships

Teaching is one of the most relational professions in the world. Although they are a critical component of our pedagogy, sometimes we don't give a lot of thought and intention to relationships.

Educator-Child Relationships

Write a list of the children in your current class or primary care group. Can you do this from memory? If (like me), you miss someone initially, reflect on why this might be. What can you plan to do this coming week to spend more time with this child and nurture your relationship?

Return to the list of children. Next to each name, write something about them as a person. By this, I mean not as a student or even as a learner. Who are they as a person? What is something you know about their family or friends? What do you know about their likes and dislikes? Do they have a passion? Do they have pets?

Reflect on the children who are difficult to write something next to. Plan ways to learn about and spend more time with these children. For example, spend lunchtime or snacktime with them, chatting about their lives.

Child-Child Relationships

Take a week to observe through the lens of child-child relationships. Watch children engage and interact as they arrive at school. Watch them as they play at recess time. Observe them as they find a place to sit in the meeting area or decide where they want to work and play.

What child-child friendships seem strong? Which appear to be emerging? Is there anyone who doesn't seem connected to other children? How can you support this child to build relationships? For example, consider how you can support the child to enter into play with others, removing yourself once the play has taken off.

Is there a child who will only interact, play, or sit with one particular person? Consider how you can support this child to build new relationships, but in a natural and authentic way rather than forced. For example, do you know another child who shares a common interest? Maybe they both have a pet cat. You could invite them to have lunch with you and talk about their pets (and share a photo of your pet if you have one). Or ask two children who you think could potentially form a friendship to help you with a chore or job for the class or preschool, such as collecting the mail, setting up a story table, or choosing new materials for the sandpit.

Educator-Family Relationships

This exercise is similar to our reflections on the educator-child relationship. Write a list of families from memory. Can you write the parents' first names (if culturally appropriate)? Now write something that you know about each family next to their name.

Were any families difficult to recall in your mind? Why might that be? What strategies can you put in place to remedy this? It could be as simple as a five-minute telephone call home for no other reason but to connect and let them know you want to have a strong relationship and work together for the benefit of their child.

Rituals of Identity and Belonging

What do you see as rituals in your current teaching?

Ritual	Purpose	Intentions
Example: Sing a "hello" song each morning.	To build a sense of belonging to a group.	• At the beginning of the year, to help children learn each other's names. • To continue to sing "hello" songs occasionally throughout the year to strengthen the connection among children.

Will your learning culture be strengthened by new rituals? What could you introduce and why?

Remember that rituals are like routines with heart. Rituals anchor the day and bind people together in a sense of belonging. Routines are what we do without thinking or without clear intentions. What feels like a routine now? What are you doing because you've always done it?

Are some routines driving the day without a sense of purpose or intentionality? Can these be changed or replaced or enhanced? Can you bring more intentionality and meaning to these routines?

Record your ideas here. (You don't have to have something in every section, but the more you fill in, the more you can consider all possibilities.)

Rituals for . . .	Notes and Actions
Identity as a group	
Celebration	
Transition	
Other rituals	

Language of Agency

What language do you already use intentionally? Why? How does it build and honor children's agency in their learning?

Words	Intention

Praise versus Encouragement

Reflect on the words you use to give feedback to children. How do they make the learning process visible?

What words will you intentionally choose to give feedback and encouragement, rather than "good job" praise? Refer to the ideas in chapter 4.

Nonverbal Language

Reflect on how often you require children to raise their hands to speak. Could this be accidentally stifling some children's voices?

When can you try a No Hands Up strategy? How will you introduce it in a small way and build on success? (For example: use pop-stick names initially so that children know this is a time when they don't need to raise their hands and wait to be chosen, or teach how to Turn and Talk with a partner.)

Environments for Agency

Temporal Environment

Write down the flow of your typical day. How many minutes are spent in teacher-initiated or teacher-directed experiences and how many in child-initiated or child-directed pursuits?

Teacher-Initiated/Directed	Child-Initiated/Directed
Approx. minutes:	Approx. minutes:

What does this reveal about the balance of experiences? Will you make any changes to ensure most of the time is spent providing opportunities for children to use their agency and initiate their own learning?

Physical Environment

How can you deinstitutionalize your space?

Deinstitutionalizing Considerations	Reflections and Plans
Lighting	
Furniture and desks	
Commercial charts	
Color	
Texture and natural materials	
Clutter and storage	
Walls	
Other	

All-Access Pass

How can you ensure children have access to materials when and where they need them?

Materials	Reflections and Plans
Mark-making tools (markers, pencils, paint, and so on)	
Tape, scissors, and glue	
Loose parts	
Symbolic play props	
Paper	
Other	

How can you ensure children have access to water and bathrooms when their bodies tell them they need it?

Learning Contexts for Agency

We can think of the characteristics of contexts for agency as each being on a continuum. This is far more helpful than seeing a learning context as either having agency or not. Choose two or three learning contexts that you plan, prepare, and propose to children. Reflect honestly about how each characteristic helps the context provide opportunities for children to use their agency and initiate their own learning. There are no right or wrong answers. If I used this continuum at another time, thinking of a bookmaking context in a different site, I might mark it differently. This is a tool for reflection, evaluation, and goal setting, not a pass-fail test.

For example:

Symbolic Play Props		
Context: Bookmaking		
Complex		
None	Some	A lot
Inclusive		
None	Some	A lot
Social		
None	Some	A lot
Active		
None	Some	A lot
Process-focused		
None	Some	A lot

Context:		
Complex		
None	Some	A lot
Inclusive		
None	Some	A lot
Social		
None	Some	A lot
Active		
None	Some	A lot
Process-focused		
None	Some	A lot

References

Ainsworth, M. 1967. *Infancy in Uganda: Infant Care and the Growth of Love.* Baltimore: Johns Hopkins University Press.

Bandura, A. 1977. "Self-Efficacy: Toward a Unifying Theory of Behavioral Change." *Psychological Review* 84, no. 2, 191–215.

Best, J. R. 2010. "Effects of Physical Activity on Children's Executive Function: Contributions of Experimental Research on Aerobic Exercise." *Developmental Review* 30, no. 4, 331–51. https://doi.org/10.1016/j.dr.2010.08.001.

Calderon, J. 2020. "Executive Function in Children: Why It Matters and How to Help." Harvard Health Publishing. Last modified December 16, 2020. www.health.harvard.edu/blog/executive-function-in-children-why-it-matters-and-how-to-help-2020121621583.

Council of Australian Governments. 2009. *Belonging, Being, and Becoming: The Early Years Learning Framework for Australia.* Canberra, Australia: Council of Australian Governments. www.acecqa.gov.au/sites/default/files/2020-05/belonging_being_and_becoming_the_early_years_learning_framework_for_australia.pdf.

Csikszentmihalyi, M. 1979. "The Concept of Flow." In *Play and Learning,* edited by B. Sutton-Smith, 257–73. New York: Gardner.

Economic and Social Research Council. 2007. "Children Stressed Six Months before Starting School." *Science Daily,* September 5, 2007. www.sciencedaily.com/releases/2007/08/070831093902.htm.

Edwards, C. P., L. Gandini, and G. E. Forman. 1993. *The Hundred Languages of Children: The Reggio Emilia Approach to Early Childhood Education.* Norwood, NJ: Ablex.

Gillespie, L., and S. Petersen. 2012. "Rituals and Routines: Supporting Infants and Toddlers and Their Families." *Young Children* 67, no. 4, pages 76–77.

Greenman, J. 2005. *Caring Spaces, Learning Places.* 2nd ed. Lincoln, NE: Exchange Press.

Jackson, P. 1990. *Life in Classrooms.* New York: Teachers College Press.

Johnston, P., et al. 2020. *Engaging Literate Minds: Developing Children's Social, Emotional, and Intellectual Lives, K–3.* Moorabbin, Australia: Hawker Brownlow.

Laevers, F. 2005. "Deep-Level-Learning and the Experiential Approach to Early Childhood and Primary Education." Katholieke Universiteit Leuven, Research Centre for Early Childhood and Primary Education. www.speelsleren.nl/wp-content/uploads/2015/05/Deep-level-learning-Ferre-Laevers.pdf.

Mooney, C. G. 2010. *Theories of Attachment: An Introduction to Bowlby, Ainsworth, Gerber, Brazelton, Kennell, and Klaus.* St. Paul, MN: Redleaf Press.

Pink, D. 2011. *Drive: The Surprising Truth about What Motivates Us.* New York: Riverhead.

Reid, A. 2019. *Changing Australian Education: How Policy Is Taking Us Backwards and What Can Be Done about It.* New York: Routledge.

Roberts, R. 2010. *Wellbeing from Birth.* London: Sage.

Robinson, K. 2006. "Do Schools Kill Creativity?" TED video. www.ted.com/talks/sir_ken_robinson_do_schools_kill_creativity.

UNICEF Australia. n.d. *A Simplified Version of the United Nations Convention on the Rights of the Child.* New South Wales: Unicef Australia. www.unicef.org.au/united-nations-convention-on-the-rights-of-the-child.

Vygotsky, L. 1978. *Mind in Society.* Cambridge, MA: Harvard University Press.

Index

Page numbers in *italics* indicate diagrams.